# APPLYING ARTIFICIAL INTELLIGENCE IN PROJECT MANAGEMENT

# APPLYING ARTIFICIAL
# INTELLIGENCE IN
# PROJECT MANAGEMENT

PAUL BOUDREAU

MERCURY LEARNING AND INFORMATION
Boston, Massachusetts

Publisher: David Pallai
MERCURY LEARNING AND INFORMATION
121 High Street, 3rd Floor
Boston, MA 02110
info@merclearning.com
www.merclearning.com
800-232-0223

P. Boudreau. *Applying Artificial Intelligence in Project Management.*
ISBN: 978-1-50152-270-3

The publisher recognizes and respects all marks used by companies, manufacturers, and developers as a means to distinguish their products. All brand names and product names mentioned in this book are trademarks or service marks of their respective companies. Any omission or misuse (of any kind) of service marks or trademarks, etc. is not an attempt to infringe on the property of others.

Library of Congress Control Number: 2024943333

242526321   This book is printed on acid-free paper in the United States of America.

Our titles are available for adoption, license, or bulk purchase by institutions, corporations, etc. For additional information, please contact the Customer Service Dept. at 800-232-0223 (toll free).

All of our titles are available in digital format at academiccourseware.com and other digital vendors. *Selected case studies for this title are available with proof of purchase by contacting info@merclearning.com.* The sole obligation of MERCURY LEARNING AND INFORMATION to the purchaser is to replace the files, based on defective materials or faulty workmanship, but not based on the operation or functionality of the product.

# CONTENTS

# PREFACE

Projects are notoriously late, over budget, and difficult to manage. This book is not about finding why projects fail but finding ways to make them successful. We live in a project economy where close to 100 million people will be performing project work and the value of project activities will reach 20 trillion dollars by 2027. Projects are at the heart of the greatest human accomplishments, whether constructing a new supply of electricity, finding a cure for a disease, or planning for humans to survive on Mars. The high failure rate and poor project performance detract from the product or service produced. A more intense focus is required on how to significantly improve project success. Artificial intelligence (AI) technology is the opportunity to achieve extraordinary improvement in project performance. Project managers need to lead the change for AI to become an integral part of the project methodology. The world needs projects to succeed, and AI technology can make that happen. Deploying AI in project management requires a knowledge of AI fundamentals, which are the foundation for current and future AI development.

Data management is a critical element in AI technology. Data is essential for all software, but even more so for AI-based machine learning algorithms. It is important to understand how software depends on data and can only achieve results when the data is properly managed. A practical approach is required to prepare and use data. Concepts such as structured data, data wrangling, and feature engineering are critical for AI deployments.

AI solutions are being deployed now for project management, and it is important to understand how these solutions work and how they improve project performance. The fundamentals of AI are based on machine learning methods such as supervised learning, unsupervised learning, and reinforcement learning. Understanding how these three main methods work also provides knowledge of how implementing AI in project management produces results. This is the most important content in the book because it outlines information critical for deploying AI and being able to interact knowledgeably with AI software vendors.

The other major AI component, natural language processing (NLP), is at the forefront of human interactions with AI and offers significant productivity gains. The main capabilities include document analysis, sentiment analysis, translation, and interaction with a virtual assistant. Each area has specific software that is useful when managing projects. Combining machine learning and natural language processing has produced generative AI. This software development is a significant opportunity to improve project performance. There are techniques for being more productive when interacting with generative AI and delivering effective results. Generative AI brings an unexpectedly high level of expertise to project management. It can also produce incomprehensible responses. Another AI-based software concept is genetic algorithms. These are algorithms designed to represent the recombination process of genes and are based on the theory of evolution. Genetic algorithms have some interesting and unique applications that might lead the next wave of advances in machine learning.

Project processes are at the heart of organizing and leading a project. Therefore, it is essential to view AI from the perspective of project processes. Reviewing processes can stimulate thoughts about how AI fits into the project methodology. Regardless of the project type, all project processes can be aided by applying AI. Perhaps the current methods for managing projects should be thrown away, and AI should be allowed to find a customized process solution that fits the project type, size, and purpose. To obtain value from a project, project managers must address all project issues while monitoring changes to the business case used to justify the project. What is a problem that could prevent project success? Can the project manager determine how AI can provide a better solution? Project managers should spend more time planning because good planning results in smoother implementation. Unfortunately, project managers do not always have the time or resources for better planning. AI can be applied to the scope, budget, schedule, and other critical project processes, resulting in greater efficiency and improved project performance.

Project control provides metrics that may prompt a project manager to take corrective action. AI improves the accuracy of metrics and analyzes trends. Earned value management metrics become more valuable when analyzed by AI software. AI knowledge should convince project managers to rethink how project closure is performed. Are the lessons learned effective? In project closure, the most critical task to make AI effective is verifying all data is captured, adequately formatted, stored, and made accessible as updates for the machine learning algorithms. Since projects are managed using different methods, a review of Agile processes is necessary. AI has an impact on improving all aspects of an Agile methodology.

There are two options for acquiring AI solutions. AI software can be created by the organization or purchased from a vendor. Understanding the fundamentals of AI provides an opportunity to communicate effectively with AI developers and vendor representatives. The basic AI components are common for most AI software, and the challenge is to discover how they apply to the project environment. There are different strategies and suggestions for implementing AI solutions. The capabilities may vary, and no single software program can be expected to solve all project problems. An important aspect for all AI software is proper implementation. Similar to achieving success in any project, applying AI to the project methodology must be carefully managed. There are pitfalls to avoid, and the project manager must use a practical approach.

The roles in project management change as AI is introduced into the project process. Some changes are apparent, and others can be forecasted based on knowledge of AI and the continuing evolution of new technology. Project practitioners must use change management to ensure AI-based software is accepted, properly implemented, and used to achieve value for the organization. AI will undoubtedly change project roles and responsibilities. For example, there are new ethical considerations for using AI-based solutions. Learning about different ethical situations and how they can be addressed in the organization is essential. AI development is evolving, and the output will become more accurate, faster, and easier to apply. AI will be combined with other technologies like blockchain, the Internet of Things (IoT), and virtual reality to create more robust solutions. Project managers must embrace AI, find creative ways to utilize the capability, and lead the change that will significantly increase project performance.

This is a pivotal moment in the history of project management. AI offers an incredible opportunity, but the technology can only provide value through knowledgeable project leaders. This is your opportunity to consider how AI can be applied to the project environment. More importantly, this is an opportunity to enjoy the feeling when AI delivers positive project results far beyond expectations.

**Paul Boudreau**
**September 2024**

# ACKNOWLEDGMENTS

Although this is roughly based on content I collected and wrote about for many years, assembling all my knowledge and experiences into a book took an incredible effort. Thanks to my wife, Jill, for her ongoing support and encouragement. My former students Anuj, Lorraine, Alex, Mikayla, and others helped me generate important ideas and concepts for applying AI to projects. Students in Canada and Europe continue to inspire me. Mila, the graphic designer, provided the images, including some for the presentations I have made around the world. My friend Andrew was a great sounding board to review concepts. His prolific data background provided valuable insight.

There are many individuals around the world promoting AI for project management. Antonio, Colin, Cuong, David, Declan, Edward, Jan Willem, Marcus, Martin, Rich, and many more continue to push for AI acceptance in project management. My college colleagues Angela and Nicole cheerfully support my ongoing work in the field.

I also must acknowledge the contribution of my friend and teaching colleague, Lathif, who is no longer with us. He was the first person to tell me several years ago that my ideas were special. I miss the lunches where he would highlight the amazing and not-so-amazing features of my most recent concept for applying AI to projects. It was always enlightening.

To all my connections around the world, I feel the momentum building. Innovation is the key to making project management an exciting and rewarding profession.

# *About the Author*

**Paul Boudreau**, MBA, PMP (Doctorate in progress), is the leading authority for applying AI to project management. His groundbreaking books have been adopted for university-level courses in Europe and North America. He is a highly respected project management professional with over thirty-five years of experience in the technology industry. Paul is a professor in Canada and Europe, teaching how to apply AI to project management. He also helps educational institutions worldwide develop courses and workshops that enhance their project management programs. Paul is a global leader in researching and applying AI concepts to project management, focusing on machine learning, natural language processing, and genetic algorithms. He published three books about using AI for project management: *Applying Artificial Intelligence to Project Management*, *How the Project Management Office Can Use Artificial Intelligence to Improve the Bottom Line*, and *The Self Driving Project: Using Artificial Intelligence to Deliver Project Success*.

Paul is a frequent speaker at project conferences and private organizations, delivering practical suggestions for deploying AI to improve project performance. He is also active in helping implement AI for project management in industry and government organizations. Considered an expert by PMI, he publishes a regular blog on pmi.org.

He is a well-known speaker who presents compelling arguments as to why AI technology has become essential to how we deliver projects.

Paul is the founder and President of Stonemeadow Consulting. In this role, he actively researches how AI technology can enhance and provide value to project management. He also works with public and private organizations to improve their project methodology.

Paul's work indicates a deep understanding of traditional project management and emerging AI technologies, positioning him as an influential voice in the field. His contributions extend from hands-on industry experience to academic research and thought leadership through his publications.

Paul lives in Ottawa, Canada.

# FUNDAMENTAL CONCEPTS OF AI IN PROJECT MANAGEMENT

This section describes the fundamental concepts of AI that are relevant to project management. Chapter 1 starts by identifying the problem in project management. Traditional methodologies are responsible for delivering disappointing project results, and even when organizations move to a mix of waterfall and Agile methods, the results do not change. Chapter 2 identifies two components of AI being implemented by organizations to improve project performance: machine learning and natural language processing. AI is not a simple single algorithm. There are a variety of AI methods, and they can be combined to deliver a solution. Chapter 3 reviews the requirement to extract value from introducing AI-based solutions. Projects have a purpose, and the funding and commitment of resources must be justified. Similarly, the value of applying AI needs to be defined. This section closes with Chapter 4, which describes the critical difference between automating project tasks and using AI.

# CHAPTER 1

# WHY PROJECT MANAGEMENT NEEDS AI

The biggest challenge for project managers is to deliver the project scope on time and on or under budget. Based on project history and easily calculated metrics, most projects are unsuccessful. Is anyone concerned? Not only are the current failure rates disappointing, but they are also incredibly wasteful and should not be tolerated. Project managers are inundated by a litany of reasons why projects fail. This is usually accompanied by various sources that offer project management training to "fix" project managers, but this approach often fails. The reason that it fails is because people are not the problem. Project managers and their teams work diligently on project tasks only to face disappointment. Projects fail due to poor project processes. There needs to be a change in "how" project management is performed. Consider the following analogy: Instead of being asked to dig a hole with bare hands, shouldn't you be allowed to use a shovel? Using this example, the "shovel" you are allowed to use represents new technology. Taking advantage of this technology is an opportunity to increase project success rates. AI software needs to transform the current project management processes so that project managers can finally be proud of achieving significantly improved project performance and higher success rates.

AI became a topic of considerable interest when an IBM computer beat the Jeopardy! television game show champion and won easily (Markoff 2011). Not only did the AI-based computer find the correct answers, but it also had perfect timing to be selected first to answer. AI has many capabilities, such as diagnosing an illness based on an x-ray image or MRI scan and using voice analysis to detect medical conditions such as post-traumatic stress disorder (Philipps 2019). The self driving car is another example of AI technology and has comparisons to project management. The self driving car has a clear objective to arrive at a destination, which requires making decisions as the vehicle progresses. Along the way, several issues are encountered and actively managed to achieve the goal. A project contains a plan, which is essentially the strategy for how to achieve the outcome. As the project is being implemented, numerous obstacles are encountered, and the correct decisions must be made to maintain progress. AI software enables the project to drive more efficiently and reach the destination on time and within the budget.

Adding AI software to the project management methodology changes how projects are managed. At the start of the project, AI software searches all project documents and looks for incomplete or misleading information. This is similar to how AI software currently looks at an x-ray image or an MRI scan and makes a diagnosis. AI can make a "diagnosis" for the project based on the "image" created with the current project documents. AI also verifies if the implementation strategy will be successful. Accessing the project documents, a prediction of project success, is made before the project starts and again as the project is being deployed. AI software helps guide and direct the project manager to make the best decisions in all situations. Ongoing predictions throughout the project highlight the ability of the project manager to keep the project on course, something that is of high interest to the project's client or sponsor. Project implementation is guided by software that optimizes resources and constantly reevaluates risks. Managing communication is no longer difficult because it is based on the psychological profiles of stakeholders, and AI software determines the best way to send clear and direct messages that motivate and inspire project stakeholders. Project issues are eliminated or minimized because they are included in a risk plan or mitigated as part of the project strategy before the project starts. The project manager can manage the project using a smartphone app with assistance and guidance from a well-trained virtual project assistant that understands project management logic and how to make all the right decisions that result in a successful project outcome. These are only some possibilities for applying AI to project management, and most are available now.

*Artificial intelligence* can be a confusing term as it encompasses many different aspects of how computer technology is used. The most appropriate meaning is the ability of computers to demonstrate some cognitive function similar to humans, such as decision-making. The software algorithms enable a multitude of new capabilities for project management due to the flexibility of the technology. We will focus on machine learning and natural language processing, the two most important components for managing projects. *Machine learning* is, in simple terms, the ability of a programmed algorithm to be trained to recognize and correlate patterns in data. For our purposes, we will use these trained algorithms to improve the success rate of projects. *Natural language processing* (NLP) is the basis for document analysis, sentiment analysis, and virtual assistants. The combination of machine learning and NLP has resulted in a powerful development known as *generative AI*.

"Machine learning" is an unusual term. The "machine" part refers to the system, such as a computer server or computer hardware, where the software is stored and the program is executed. The "learning" part is when the algorithm is trained on input data to create a model that can be used to predict or classify a new set of data. It is the algorithm that does the learning, and the machine or hardware is the place where the result is computed and stored.

The second essential component of AI, NLP, is a computer program's ability to interpret human language and classify communication into meaning or, as it is called in NLP, an *intent*. It includes the ability to evaluate the emotion behind words, which becomes part of a skill known as *sentiment analysis*. This characteristic is interesting because people use words differently and have different backgrounds. NLP searches documents, extrapolates meaning, and determines correlations and anomalies. These algorithms dramatically influence how humans interact with machines now that machines can analyze and identify human behavior and personalities. NLP is also used for language translation and the ability to communicate with a digital assistant such as Siri, Alexa, or Google Assistant.

AI is a *disruptive* technology, and, as project managers, that concept needs to be embraced. "Disruption" is a word that suggests the project process needs to be performed differently, and integrating AI software can accomplish this. AI is similar to other new technologies, requiring users to understand how to evaluate it, learn its value, and implement it properly. It is different because it is a far more complex and powerful technology and is subject to broad misunderstanding and fear. It has the potential to solve numerous problems and provide incredible value in many areas of our society, including project management. The most significant challenge of using AI for project managers is finding creative ways to apply AI and uncover the value that makes adoption more compelling.

AI changes project processes, and it certainly changes how people think about and manage projects. Some people claim AI will only "automate" tasks. That is partly true, but not in the way most people think about automation. As new AI software capabilities are developed, it becomes more apparent that projects cannot continue to be managed in the traditional way. This is a helpful observation: Imagine the benefits of much higher project success rates. Improved project performance means fewer wasted resources, increased environmental sustainability, lower stress levels for the project team, and generally more positive results and positive energy. Above all, the value of consistently completing projects on time and on or under budget is enormous, adding a new credibility factor to project delivery.

Project management is an exciting field. It is responsible for all the changes in the world because it takes a project to make a change, whether or not it is called "a project." Projects are used to implement new technology, so it is natural that project management should be the subject of new technology such as AI. A well-structured project will land people on Mars, and it will be a project that finds a cure for cancer. Yet, these incredible accomplishments cannot continue with traditional methods. It is time to inject AI into project management processes, but this will not be easy. People struggle to understand how to introduce new technologies due to the complexity of managing projects. It may not be clear where or how AI software can be implemented successfully in a project.

There are a variety of statistics on project failure rates. One survey reported that 68 percent of information technology (IT) projects fail, and 70 percent of organizations had at least one project failure in the previous 12 months (Krigsman 2009). In 2013, fewer than 33 percent of projects were completed on time and on budget, and for every one billion dollars invested in projects in the United States, $122 million was wasted due to poor project performance (PMI 2018). Whatever the source of information, the overall success rate of projects is far less than 50 percent. One study revealed that of 81 US transit projects completed between 1987 and 2018, 77 percent exceeded the original budget (Gao and Touran 2020). The history of megaprojects, which have a budget of over one billion dollars, reveals that 90 percent have cost overruns of at least 50 percent (Flyvbjerg and Gardner 2023). Project failure creates funding issues, financial loss, damage to customer trust, negative publicity, risk of deterioration to competitive advantage, and anxious project stakeholders (Yim et al. 2015). Based on any metric of project success rates, machine learning and NLP solutions for project management cannot happen quickly enough. There are an estimated 16.5 million project managers worldwide, and they need to embrace this new technology (Project.co 2023).

Project results are humanity's greatest successes. From creating pyramids to launching rockets into space, the list of completed projects shows spectacular human achievements. The list of megaprojects in the world includes a vast array of initiatives. From aerospace to a natural disaster cleanup to hosting global sports events, it is the ability to complete a project that demonstrates human progress. The purpose of a project is to create something new or achieve a result that has not been accomplished previously. Projects are the drivers of change in the world. Functional management is an operation that is repeated on a regular basis. It is far easier to implement machine learning software into functional management because the same activities happen on a regular basis. Not only is every project different, but the process used to implement projects varies greatly. The Project Management Institute (PMI) uses the Project Management Body of Knowledge (PMBOK) as a guide for project managers. Anyone who has worked on different projects realizes that it would be useful to have a common process, but it rarely happens. Organizations have difficulty fully implementing a structured project methodology such as Waterfall, and the same is true for using Agile to perform software development. It should be no surprise that the predominant project methodology is a hybrid of both processes (Nieto-Rodriguez 2021). Organizations select what they think is best from each process, and, unfortunately, they are not always right. Why not use AI to make that choice? There are probably few effective standard project processes, and only by using AI can the process be optimized. AI determines a customized process that delivers a successful result for each project type and size. Project methodologies vary widely by industry. They might have common issues such as risk and resource planning, but by using AI, each project finds a project process or methodology that works for their project. Some projects have no predetermined process at all. Implementing machine learning software may be more challenging in this type of project environment.

As projects adopt some of the AI software used in a functional setting, such as organizing a meeting or capturing meeting action items, some efficiencies will be achieved for project managers. An AI software program automatically creates a status report or identifies the most efficient resources for a task. These are incremental gains, and project management needs significant improvements. Project management needs software that will increase the project success rate to 95 percent or higher on a consistent basis. There are high expectations for applying AI to project management, and implementation is underway. The ultimate benefit is an accurate scope, budget, and schedule to complete the project with a full list and mitigation plan for potential risks. Customers and project sponsors will know that selecting and starting a project means delivering the expected result. AI also delivers more efficient projects as productivity increases. Can project managers find a way to adopt the software that will significantly improve project results? AI is a new and complex technology. Project managers need to be knowledgeable enough to understand the concepts and technical knowledge and be creative enough to find ways to insert the right solutions into the process.

For organizations that already have a strong success rate in projects, the formula will change. Projects are becoming more complex, and the environment is becoming more complicated. The world of work is becoming personalized, customized, and globalized. Success today does not guarantee success in the future, so the continuation of a winning project implementation methodology still requires changes that will have a positive impact on the outcome.

## QUESTIONS

### Review questions

1. Why are improvements in managing projects critical to humanity?

2. Why is AI considered an opportunity in project management?

3. Describe the two main components of AI that have the most significant impact on managing projects.

### Discussion questions

1. Why do some organizations use a hybrid process instead of Waterfall or Agile?

2. Will the desire for short term productivity improvements distract organizations from applying AI to significantly change project methods?

3. If an organization resolves all the reasons why a project failed, does this guarantee future success?

## REFERENCES

Brame, A., Cumming, S., Barlow, G., Avery, G., &and Woolley, P. (2010) KPMG New Zealand project management survey 2010, *https:// home.kpmg/nz/en/home/insights.htmlhttps://home.kpmg/nz/en/ home/insights.html*

Crear, J. (2019). The Standish Group Report: *Chaos, https://www. projectsmart.co.uk/whitepapers/chaos-report.pdf*

Flyvbjerg, B. and Gardner, D. (2023). *How big things get done: The surprising factors that determine the fate of every project, from home renovations to space exploration and everything in between.* New York: Crown Currency.

Gao, N., and Touran, A. (2020). Cost overruns and formal risk assessment program in US rail transit projects. *Journal of Construction Engineering and Management, 146*(5), 05020004.

Krigsman, M. (2009). Study: 68% of projects fail, *ZDNet*, January 14, 2009, *https://www.zdnet.com/article/study-68-percent-of-it-projects-fail/https://www.zdnet.com/article/study-68-percent-of-it-projects-fail/*

Markoff, J. (2011). Computer wins on Jeopardy!: Trivial it's not, *N.Y.Y. Times*. Retrieved December 22, 2023.

Nieto-Rodriguez, A. (2021). *Harvard business review project management handbook: how to launch, lead, and sponsor successful projects*. Harvard Business Press. *https://www.nytimes. com/2011/02/17/science/17jeopardy-watson.htmlhttps://www. nytimes.com/2011/02/17/science/17jeopardy-watson.html*

Philipps, D. (2019). The military wants better tests for PTSD. Speech analysis could be the answer. *The New York Times Magazine*, April 19, *https://www.nytimes.com/2019/04/22/magazine/veterans-ptsd-speech-analysis.html*.

Project Management Institute (PMI), (2018). Pulse of the profession survey, *https://www.pmi.org/about/press-media/press-releases/2018-pulse-of-the-profession-survey*

*Project management statistics: Everything you need to know*. Project. co, retrieved December 22, 2023. *https://www.project.co/project-management-statistics/#:~:text=There%20are%20an%20estimated%2016.5%20million%20project%20managers%20in%20the%20worldhttps://www.project.co/project-management-statistics/#:~:text=There%20are%20an%20estimated%2016.5%20million%20project%20managers%20in%20the%20world*.

University of Vermont. (2019) AI can detect depression in a child's speech. *ScienceDaily*. Retrieved September 8, 2019, *https://www. sciencedaily.com/releases/2019/05/190506150126.htm*

Yim, R., Castaneda, J., Doolen, T., Tumer, I., & and Malak, R. (2015). A study of the impact of project classification on project risk indicators. *International Journal of Project Management*, 33(4), 863–876. *https://doi.org/10.1016/j.ijproman.2014.10.005https://doi.org/10.1016/j.ijproman.2014.10.005*

# TWO AI COMPONENTS FOR PROJECTS

The two primary components of AI for managing projects are machine learning and natural language processing. They are used separately to solve project issues, but can be combined to create generative AI, which provides a vast array of responses when interacting with project management practitioners. Project managers need to learn the fundamental characteristics of these components to become more effective in delivering successful projects.

## MACHINE LEARNING

The ultimate objective of machine learning is to use the data to do one of two things: prediction or classification. At its core, the algorithm uses a mathematical formula based on calculus to find the least error between correlations in the data. This is also known as *minimizing the cost function*. Machine learning is not an expert system or a simulator. Simulation software excels at running multiple scenarios, allowing a selection of the best one or one with the greatest probability of success. AI or machine learning software looks at the same data and develops a correlation that may be too complex for a human brain to determine. From that correlation, and assuming there is enough training data, the software makes a prediction. A simulation determines several possible outcomes or the most likely outcome. The advantage of AI is accuracy. The disadvantage is the need to have an appropriate amount of training data to make a valid prediction. The advantage of a simulation is that it gives a range of possibilities based on the available data. The disadvantage is that it does not make a prediction, only illustrating the variety of possible successful outcomes. Both use statistical methods, but the AI algorithm learns from the data by making correlations that improve the result.

Machine learning software is created using a programming language, such as Python. It uses utilities or libraries to develop learning algorithms, with the most common and effective one being a neural network. A *neural network* is a software representation of how neurons perform in a human brain. The software is not a human brain and has no chemical or biological components. The software code performs the statistical correlation required in regression analysis. There are three common learning methods for an AI algorithm.

*Supervised learning* is where a dataset is labeled, and the algorithm is trained to correlate each dataset with the labeled result. The algorithm iteratively adjusts the coefficients in the correlation model, fine-tuning them to achieve the highest level of accuracy. This process continues until the model reaches an optimal configuration that best fits the data. The result is then used on test data to verify the model's accuracy. Supervised learning is used in health care to diagnose x-ray images and can provide higher accuracy than a trained technician (Armitage 2018). First, the algorithm is trained on x-ray images labeled as showing evidence or no evidence of a condition. Next, a new x-ray image is provided for input to the algorithm, and AI diagnoses or predicts the result. For projects, the datasets are labeled based on project conditions. For example, several characteristics, known as *features* in machine learning language, are captured for each project. The projects are labeled a success or failure based on a predetermined definition. The definition can change but must be applied consistently to each dataset. (An example is explained more clearly in an upcoming chapter.) For now, any project dataset can be labeled. There are successful projects, well-executed risk plans, and communication plans that result in high stakeholder satisfaction. There are also negative results for each example.

*Unsupervised learning* occurs when the datasets are not labeled, but the algorithm can classify the dataset effectively with sufficient clues. The main benefit of unsupervised learning is *clustering*, which occurs when the algorithm groups similar items together based on certain characteristics. For example, the algorithm can practice by sorting types of fruit: Based on the size, color, and weight, the software program separates bananas, apples, and oranges into groups. This type of approach to sorting is frequently used in recommender systems, where a person likes a specific book or film and the algorithm looks at similar books or movies and recommends purchasing them. How is this approach applied to projects? Risks are clustered or grouped so that when one of the risks from a cluster occurs, there is a strong possibility that a similar risk will occur. If one type of problem occurs in an organization, then it may be likely that problems that are classified as similar will also happen. Another possibility is determining which risks are missing in a group or which risks need to be added. Do risk clusters have a common cause? If so, the project manager can take action to proactively address the cause. The risks might also be addressed by using a common mitigation strategy.

The process of assessing items in a group and assuming they have the same attributes is called *semi-supervised learning* and offers additional capability for machine learning algorithms. In evaluating a group of items, one is labeled and the others are not. The label for the single item is attributed to the similar items surrounding it. An example is to group project tasks by complexity. Finding a group of tasks that has high complexity is helpful for project planning. If 80 percent of the tasks are high complexity, the project manager needs to reassess the skills for the allocated resources. Perhaps further training is required, or an expert can be acquired to share experience and knowledge to overcome the level of complexity required. In this example, a machine learning algorithm is used to avoid project issues that threaten project success.

*Reinforcement learning* is a process of making decisions based on avoiding previous mistakes. Humans interact with the world, learning the decisions and actions needed to achieve goals. Learning to ride a bicycle requires balance and steering to avoid falling over. In machine learning, reinforcement learning is an algorithm that learns to make the correct decision through trial and error. In the world of project management, this is called *experience*. Similar to gaining experience, the AI-based algorithm uses historical data. Reinforcement learning algorithms can start with no data and gradually become experts by learning from mistakes (for example, as in a game such as chess). However, this may not be the best strategy for managing a project. A typical example is typing on a smartphone, where the whole word appears after only typing two or three letters. The program learns a person's pattern through repetitions where the suggested word is not selected. The learning process is apparent with uncommon words or a business name such as "Stonemeadow," which is unusual and not in a dictionary. The person ignores the recommendation to use "stonemason" or some other variation and types in the word correctly. On the second try, the smartphone again recommends different endings. On the third attempt, the smartphone learns that the most likely word is "Stonemeadow," and after typing the first few letters, it correctly shows the option of the word desired.

Computers can retain a considerable amount of data and have excellent recall. Think of an issue that is captured for a project in progress. What is the problem, and how can it be solved? Project managers gather data and think about possible solutions. Reinforcement learning is used in this situation to avoid a solution that has failed in the past. Now, think about having a database that contains all the decisions for a similar issue in numerous previous projects. The project manager avoids decisions that do not work and tries a new solution. If the new solution is successful, the reward is feeling good about making the correct decision.

## NATURAL LANGUAGE PROCESSING (NLP)

Natural language processing (NLP) is used for document analysis, sentiment analysis, and translation, and it is utilized by virtual assistants. NLP starts with a concept called *tokenization*, which simply means parsing all the words into separate items known as *tokens*. One concept used after tokenization is referred to as a *bag of words*. The software takes a paragraph and counts the instances for each unique word. If there are ten instances of the word "happy" and one instance of the word "confused," the paragraph is classified as having a positive sentiment. How is this useful? The project manager hosts a project kickoff meeting, and after the meeting, project team member messages contain words such as "confused," "frustrated," or "unclear." The project manager takes action to improve communication and clarify the project objectives and team responsibilities.

Further development enabled NLP software to identify parts of speech such as verbs, nouns, and adjectives; it can also identify proper nouns, known as *named entities*. There are preprogrammed libraries that determine parts of speech for different languages. This tagging process is important for language translation because words have different meanings depending on how they are used. *Recurrent neural networks* (RNNs) are a method to process sentences, becoming powerful translation software. One of the challenges in project management is to ensure that the content is compared to project management vocabulary. Some terms in project management have a different meaning from general speech, such as a "critical path" or "earned value." Determining sentiment for a project environment needs to account for a subset of language that contains project jargon.

NLP is used in document analysis to determine consistency in a specification such as a scope document. This type of software discovers errors and omissions. The scope can define the requirement for a deliverable, but the document may not include testing the deliverable. Techniques are available to produce a preliminary cost and schedule estimate based on the scope of the content. Sentiment analysis can also analyze human expression to detect conditions such as excitement, frustration, or disappointment. Sentiment analysis is an opportunity to improve the project communication plan and interactions with stakeholders. Translation is useful for globally dispersed projects. A virtual assistant allows for a verbal interaction between a project manager and AI-based software. This is commonly used in smartphones and smart home devices. The conversational interchange is important for project management and the ability to use a growing technology known as generative AI.

Generative AI is a combination of natural language processing and machine learning. Large language models (LLMs) such as ChatGPT, Google Gemini, and Llama use a method called *transformers*, which is an architecture that uses a large volume of documents to generate accurate and human-like responses to queries. The value for project management organizations is applying the generative pretrained transformers (GPT) software to the organization's own project database or a shared project database. The response to questions is faster and more accurate than any project team member can provide. If the project manager asks, "How can the schedule be reduced by one week without increasing the project cost?," the response is based on a much larger volume of projects than a single project manager's experience. As in many situations with technology, caution is required to ensure the answer resolves the project issue.

## AI BACKGROUND

The work in AI began decades ago, and some concepts are still relevant today. In an article published in 1950, Alan Turing proposed the concept that machine learning software does not have to be a perfectly complete model as long as it can be taught how to learn (Turing 1950). This concept is essential for successful AI in all areas and cannot be forgotten when using AI software for project management. While other software applications require version upgrades, machine learning software requires data upgrades. In other words, a machine learning algorithm cannot be deployed and then ignored. A feedback loop is required, and there needs to be an ongoing input of fresh data that supports the training process to maintain accurate results (O'Neil 2016). Software and data updates are essential in preserving machine learning algorithms to ensure the software continues producing proper results. AI software that starts as a child needs more attention to learn and make good decisions.

There are two streams of AI. One is *narrow AI*, which focuses on achieving a specific objective, and the other is *strong AI*, known as artificial general intelligence (AGI) or whole-brain emulation (Bostrom 2016). Artificial general intelligence is the concept that generates fear based on how it is portrayed in fiction, where a computer becomes more intelligent than humans and takes over the world. An algorithm that performs all functions is conceptually possible but has numerous practical difficulties. As with humans, AI needs resources to continue, which are not free. Even if the kind of AGI found in the science fiction movies is never achieved, amazing discoveries may occur along the way. Generative AI can be mistaken for AGI, but it really performs narrow AI over many fields. AGI is the ability to develop concepts and make discoveries that humans have not yet achieved.

Project management must identify the value for either a narrow or general AI model when deploying machine learning software. Can a single model be developed that determines how to achieve project success for all projects, regardless of size, function, and purpose? Solutions are more likely to use narrow AI, with a practical approach using machine learning algorithms and NLP.

## SOFTWARE CONCEPTS

Machine learning software is based on calculus. Machine learning algorithms are typically coded in a programming language such as R, Python, or Java. Python is an easy-to-learn, free, open-source programming language. It is concise, powerful, and has numerous standard libraries or utilities that contain pre-written code. Python is a preferred language for developing machine learning algorithms because it is simple to learn, has excellent data handling capacity, and includes complex mathematical equations in the standard libraries.

One important feature of software code, for those unfamiliar with the basic concepts, is that it can use loops that repeatedly execute the same command. This means a function can be performed repeatedly for a specified number of times or until a condition is met. Here is a simple example of a "for" loop in Python.

```
for i in range (1, 20):
    print df.loc[i]
```

This loop repeats 20 times, printing each character in the range, then stops. A machine learning algorithm uses a loop until the function achieves a specified condition. Inside the loop is an equation that attempts to optimize correlations in data.

In Figure 2.1, the highest point is on the left side of the curve, and the algorithm moves down the curve mathematically until it finds the lowest point. The machine learning algorithm used to do this is called *gradient descent*, which minimizes the error in a correlation between two variables. Another way to think of this is that it is optimizing the correlation between variables. In a neural network, there are many variables with many of these curves, and this technique is used to adjust the model. The learning part is the algorithm finding the optimum correlation, which is then used for classification or prediction. Fortunately, the algorithms for performing this function can be accessed from a library in Python.

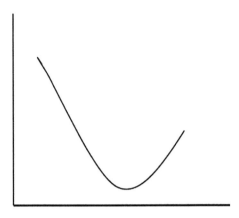

**FIGURE 2.1** Gradient descent

To work properly, a neural network uses processes known as forward propagation and backpropagation to adjust the parameters known as weights and biases so that the result is the best fit for the model created. What is being correlated? In a supervised learning model, the input data for the number of datasets is correlated to the label assigned to each dataset. A programmed loop repeats the training process for a specified number of times, known as *epochs*, to make further adjustments to the weights and biases, creating a more accurate model.

Figure 2.2 shows how the algorithm learns to make the proper correlations based on numerous iterations of adjusting weights and biases.

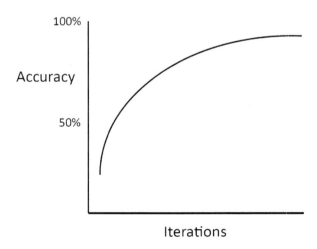

**FIGURE 2.2** Using iterations to improve supervised learning accuracy

More details about this process can be found by checking the definitions of the terms, searching reliable Web sites, and investigating the appropriate books and introductory courses dedicated to the subject. This is not a complete explanation and is only an attempt to illustrate that the algorithm has a mathematical basis for calculating results.

## CRITICISMS OF ARTIFICIAL INTELLIGENCE

It can be difficult to accept new technologies, especially when they are arriving at an increasing speed and frequency. The massive array of AI variations can frustrate and confuse people. Project managers need to provide leadership in regards to rapid technological change. Project managers need to acquire more knowledge to understand the software, ensure programs are selected that provide value for the way projects are managed, and find a way to ensure stakeholders accept the new AI-enabled processes to implement the software successfully. That is a significant challenge.

There is reason to be cautious with AI software because algorithms have the potential to cause harm. Software designers must find a way to address this concern. Historical data only represents the past. Although humanity has advanced and is adopting concepts such as universal human rights, machine learning software has a natural tendency to give current standards lower value in consideration of the vast amount of historical data. Results derived from data with considerable bias often contain a *hidden bias*. For example, an organization may want to achieve gender equality in the workplace, but the historical data may distort the results produced by the software because of past inequities. For example, machine learning software will be trained to recommend a male CEO for a construction company if that has been the most common historical result. Historical data can promote stereotypes and may contain assumptions that certain people are incapable of changing their behavior or beliefs, leading to inaccurate evaluations of the datasets. Project managers need to be aware of the existence of hidden bias and view it as a serious issue.

Another danger for AI software is when it is created to provide a specific function and then abandoned. For example, consider an elevator that is installed in a new building. It works perfectly at first, but over time, with the lack of proper maintenance or repair, it becomes less valuable and possibly even fatal to the people it is trying to help. The same is true for machine learning algorithms. They need maintenance in the form of updates and the ability to grow and develop based on new data.

## QUESTIONS

### Review questions

1. How is supervised learning different from unsupervised learning?

2. Why is data necessary for reinforcement learning?

3. What are the different capabilities of NLP, and how can they help project managers?

### Discussion questions

1. What areas of project management can benefit from being able to make a prediction?

2. What project management problems can take advantage of unsupervised learning?

3. How much data is required for reinforcement learning to be useful?

4. Who should be responsible for avoiding the dangers of AI?

## REFERENCES

Armitage, H. (2018). X-ray results can provide higher accuracy than a trained technician, *Medical Xpress*, 11(18), *https://medicalxpress.com/news/2018-11-ai-outperformedradiologists-screening-x-rays.html*

Bostrom, N. (2016). *Superintelligence: Paths, Dangers, Strategies.* Oxford University Press.

O'Neil, C. (2016). *Weapons of Math Destruction: How Big Data Increases Inequality and Threatens Democracy*, Broadway Books.

Turing, A. (1950). Computer machinery and intelligence, *Mind, LIX (236).*

# CHAPTER 3

# THE BUSINESS CASE FOR AI

N umerous examples outside of project management demonstrate the successful implementation of AI software and how the business or organization received a significant benefit. In a survey by Deloitte, 11 percent of organizations reported a return of investment from AI of over 40 percent, and another 12 percent reported returns of 30 percent or more (Loucks et al. 2019). The value is usually expressed in increased revenue or bottom-line cost savings. The value of deploying AI software for project management must also be captured in a business case. Two identifiable benefits of using AI in project management are

- productivity
- decision-making

Productivity gains occur from creating accurate project documents and creating them much faster than a human project manager. Developing a communication plan or reviewing project plans for errors is accomplished quickly using generative AI. Productivity gains improve project efficiency, but are not likely to change project outcomes. Delivering the project scope by the scheduled completion date and within the budget requires decisions. Applying AI to decision-making offers significant value.

The easiest way to express value is to identify the benefit of increasing the project success rates in the organization. To capture the financial impact, a review of past projects that failed to meet the schedule or budget can be completed. The delays and budget overspending can be quantified and used to justify the cost of acquiring AI software. Some projects incur penalties for missing schedule deadlines. Additional benefits can be found by quantifying the reduction in waste and resources that could have been better utilized or reassigned to more productive activities. It is more difficult to quantify the improved motivation of project team members with greater confidence in the project process. There is value in having an organization that consistently achieves goals such as meeting schedule deadlines and preparing accurate project budgets. The client or sponsor of projects will favor project organizations and project teams that know how to win. Calculating the value of a business benefit is always easier to determine than the value of a human benefit, such as reducing stress or improving communications. Projects may also have some positive environmental aspects due to higher success rates.

Acquiring AI software to improve the project methodology requires an analysis of costs compared to the value received by completing the project. The business case for implementing AI software seems straightforward but has significant challenges. Generally, any software that improves the project schedule or reduces project cost provides value to an organization. Calculating the costs for implementation requires a more intense review. Most organizations face two serious implementation issues when calculating the deployment cost: data and single focus.

1. *Data.* Experience in AI deployment projects shows that 60 to 80 percent of the initial effort is acquiring and cleaning data (Press 2016). Therefore, the business case must include the cost of creating and implementing a data management strategy for project data. Typical data issues include a one-time cost to clean existing data and an ongoing cost to maintain clean data. An organization may require a data architect to help define data standards and ongoing strategies to properly maintain the project data.

2. *Single focus.* Implementing AI software to perform a single activity in project management is problematic because projects are integrated across several knowledge areas. AI software that compresses schedule duration by two weeks also needs to consider the side effects on risk, quality, and other areas across the project. Project professionals understand the triangle of project baselines: scope, budget, and schedule. When one is altered, one or both sides of

the triangle are affected. Many AI software solutions in project management have a single purpose, so any unforeseen negative results and remediation must be considered for the business case. AI-based software can still perform a valuable function in a single area of project management. The caution is to understand if there are any unforeseen implications in other areas of the project. A project manager is responsible for considering all aspects of the project when making decisions.

Single-focus AI software may cause project issues, but it is still worth your consideration. For example, consider the effort it takes for several people to evaluate an extensive request for proposal (RFP) document to decide whether to bid on the work. Machine learning software using NLP can review the document and recommend an acceptable bid. That, in turn, allows an appropriate decision to be made. Any activity that requires that a significant number of resources be consumed with reading and analyzing documents on a project can be done faster and more accurately using AI. Single-focus AI software can also review a scope statement for completeness or inaccuracies. Capturing errors early in documents is a valuable cost-saving since finding errors due to misleading or inaccurate documents is more costly as the project progresses (CISQ 2022).

While the cost of AI software is added to a business case, it should be noted that one machine learning algorithm can be used for many solutions. This means that the price is for a reusable software algorithm, and the cost can be distributed as it is applied to additional areas. A pay-per-use or subscriber-based cost model is common in procuring software, and this model can be expected to continue with AI software.

For project managers, creating a good business case is a significant achievement. The business case justifies the project, motivates the team, and provides a clear objective. A well-constructed business case typically considers all costs, although some of those costs are less obvious for AI deployments.

Typical benefits of using AI in project management include the following:

- consistent on-time completion
- consistently within the budget

- greater efficiency and reduced waste

- improved productivity for project administration and planning

- optimized resource allocation

- environmental benefits

- improved stakeholder satisfaction

- competitive advantage

The costs of deploying AI software include the following:

- data management

- software usage cost

- training

- ongoing support and maintenance

- change management

## MISUNDERSTANDINGS OF AI

There are many types of electronic and programmed devices, but AI is different from these. It has a "cognitive" ability that is unique, and this ability has resulted in the creation of misleading language and ideas about AI systems. Because of this misunderstanding about AI, its use can evoke feelings of anxiety. AI is basically an algorithmic system that uses data to learn, make predictions, and classify information. For example, a self driving car uses AI. The machine learning logic makes decisions based on various streams of real-time information. An appliance like a dishwasher, however, is not an example of AI. Not all examples of AI technologies are so easily defined, though. For example, a robotic arm on an assembly line is not AI: Its logic is preprogrammed and does not change unless there is a manual intervention to adjust the program. Software programs that read x-ray images and determine a diagnosis more accurately than a technician are AI. The AI system was trained on large datasets of x-ray and other medical information in order to recognize and classify patterns. Perhaps the distinction is sometimes unclear because many people believe that any device that replaces the capability of a human should be considered AI.

AI systems can learn and make decisions based on the data they are given, and these functions can be very humanlike and quite clever. However, not all clever solutions have "intelligence." Consider the following example. If a person decides to clean a house and pulls out an old vacuum cleaner from the 1980s, some have a feature called a "smart" cord. The cord is pulled out to any desired length and stays that length while vacuuming. When finished and trying to reel in the cord, a retract button is pressed. The spring inside the cord caddy is activated, and the cord automatically spins itself back into the cord compartment. That is very clever, but is it "smart?" Does it have "intelligence?" Unfortunately, some marketers like to assign attention-grabbing words to products and ideas, so caution is advised when interacting with various types of software and technologies.

## QUESTIONS

### Review questions

1. How do the benefits of AI apply to different organizations?
2. Why is change management important?

### Discussion questions

1. What are some additional costs or benefits of deploying AI?
2. How can an organization decide if the costs outweigh the benefits?

## REFERENCES

CISQ. "CISQ Publishes the Cost of Poor Software Quality in the US: A 2022 Report," (2022, December 7). *Plus, Company Updates*

Krasner, H., (2022). The Cost of Poor Software Quality in the US: A 2022 Report, CISQ, https://www.it-cisq.org/wp-content/uploads/sites/6/2022/11/CPSQ-Report-Nov-22-2.pdf

Loucks J. et al., "Future in the Balance? How Countries Are Pursuing an AI Advantage," Deloitte, May 1, 2019, *https://www2.deloitte.com/insights/us/en/focus/cognitive-technologies/ ai-investment-by-country.html*

Press G. "Cleaning Big Data: Most Time-Consuming, Least Enjoyable Data Science Task, Survey Says," Forbes, March 23, 2016, *https:// www.forbes.com/sites/gilpress/2016/03/23/ data-preparation-most-time-consuming-least-enjoyable-data-science-task-surveysays/#11ec00896f63*

# CHAPTER 4

# AUTOMATING PROJECT MANAGEMENT TASKS

The pace of technological development makes AI more practical every day. From self driving vehicles to computers that are better than humans at complex games, this technology can now access and process more information than the human brain. Project managers need to consider what changes have to take place in the project management processes and project documents to take advantage of AI's value. There are two primary opportunities for applying AI in project management: productivity and decision-making. This chapter is about productivity improvements for projects.

Project management remains a largely manual function. The project manager creates a project management plan, which includes the project schedule, risk register, stakeholder register, and numerous other documents. The project manager also reviews changes, manages a project team, and communicates with stakeholders, all of which are time-consuming activities. Project scheduling software offers a form of automation if the project start date is created and the remaining activities are coded as dependencies. The critical path and schedule end date are automatically generated.

Generative AI can automate many of a project's administrative tasks. Project documents can be generated in minutes, compared to a lengthy manual process. The documents used, though, are based on historical projects and must be verified as appropriate and complete for the project requirements. Generative AI is also useful for reviewing project documents for accuracy. Checking for errors and omissions in a lengthy scope or schedule document using generative AI takes less time and is more accurate than a human project manager (Prieto, Mengiste, and García de Soto 2023). This is a significant productivity gain for project managers.

There are numerous project management tasks that are tedious and repetitive. For many activities, such as cost estimating, the work is calculated for one project and then repeated for a new project. Can these tasks be automated? They certainly can be automated, but a more relevant issue is whether they need AI. It is possible that expert systems can automate routine tasks, although using AI techniques may improve the accuracy. Some of the automated software being implemented for functional and office managers is also being applied to the field of project management.

Software is available to automate a range of tasks, such as creating status reports or capturing and communicating meeting notes, but do these activities provide significant value to the project objectives? Perhaps automation in project management has been slow to be implemented because each project is unique, and every project has a myriad of challenges and changes that are difficult to predict. Project Management Offices (PMOs) offer templates with the intention that each project manager can produce a consistent result. The integration of project management software with the sponsoring organization's other existing software applications has the potential to help provide value, but it is also problematic. For example, time-tracking software can automatically update the project schedule by updating the time spent on an activity. Then, the project manager can use the result to compare this to the forecast. Estimating the original amount of time required for an activity and then matching it to time spent is an imperfect equation. For example, assume an estimated activity is planned to consume 40 hours with a variable of +/- 10 percent. Meanwhile, the person working on the activity submits 30 hours, which may include some non-work-related time. If there is no indication of the task being completed, how does a project manager know if the activity is complete? Based on the time submitted, is the project ahead or behind schedule? The problem with automation in the examples above is that there is no intelligence behind it, which is precisely where AI can deliver value. AI development in project management can drive automation. Without AI, the automation of activities is protracted and ineffective at achieving the required increase in project success rates. For AI, focusing on the project management process or methodology is important. Once the project plans are created, can automation increase efficiency or improve the project success rate? Project delivery tends to rely more on decision-making than continuing to automate project management tasks. Automation is a process that is repeated and is based on a fixed set of instructions. AI learns from data and makes decisions in existing or new situations. The lure of automation for project management activities can confuse organizations into implementing a process that provides far less value.

Other issues with automation and using AI result in the need for effective change management. A study sponsored by the Agile Alliance attempted to build a virtual Scrum Master using automation techniques and machine learning. The outcome was the ability to automate 40 percent of the tasks (DeSouza and Meharwade 2018). Additional observations, however, included a fear of AI capability and the change in roles. The requirements of consistency in the process forced people to become more disciplined, but then project team members became unwilling to share data. While this study may have conceded failure at automating the Scrum Master role, AI capabilities have increased in subsequent years, and so its eventual deployment is inevitable. Evidence indicates that AI significantly changes how projects are managed and places the responsibility on project managers to manage the transition effectively.

Vendors of existing project management software may not be helping the transformation that is needed by introducing AI. They are merely adding pieces of AI, like predictive analytics, to their software. This may be problematic. Consider the following example. The project completion date is delayed by three days, and now the project is forecast to be three days late. The predictive analytics software checks resource productivity and recommends that person A replace person B on specific tasks. This change will keep the project on track and recover the three days because Person B is more efficient. This sounds like a reasonable solution, but perhaps it is not. More scrutiny is required. The project manager also needs to consider the risk of this solution, as well as the quality of work from Person B. Project managers must consider all aspects of the project, yet this approach is a piecemeal solution. If you follow formal project processes, there are at least ten areas for concern: integration, scope, schedule, cost, resources, communication, quality, risk, procurement, and stakeholder management. It is essential to take a holistic or integrated approach to the project, which means that all interactions between any of these knowledge areas must be considered. Similarly, it is important that any AI software has an integrated view of the project and does not optimize one specific activity or area while ignoring the interconnected project activity.

Let's consider another example of using technology. Many businesses have implemented large enterprise resource planning (ERP) or customer relationship management (CRM) software applications such as SAP, Peoplesoft, or Microsoft Dynamics. These organizations identify and list employees' tasks and then determine which of these can be automated by the ERP system. This process usually begins by asking an employee about their tasks and then including these on a list. Then, they ask another employee about their work, make a list of those tasks, and decide those tasks must also be automated using the ERP. This continues until the company has a complete list of tasks and a plan to automate them using the ERP system. This is a questionable approach when trying to implement technology. These organizations receive little or insignificant value from deploying the technology in this manner. Other organizations use a different strategy and realize that with an ERP system, they can process work in parallel instead of sequentially. With the ERP system, they can see more data, and much of their data will be updated in real time. They redesign their business processes to take advantage of those characteristics, resulting in a significant benefit from implementing the technology. The same is true for AI software: While an organization might gain some benefits from deploying AI when automating tasks, the true value lies in developing a strategy to change the way that projects are managed.

Does automating specific tasks, such as resource scheduling or estimating, provide enough change? Some people will argue that the project management methods have to be "disrupted." For example, there may not be a need to perform detailed estimates. If AI produces a definitive estimate for cost and schedule, there is no requirement to use manually intensive estimating techniques. If it takes fifteen people three days to scan and verify a contract document, which is performed easily and faster in a couple of hours with AI software, then that is significant. The concern is when project management activities are subject to a series of improvements that get in the way of making important changes. Each incremental improvement may total 20 percent gained in productivity, but one significant change to the project method may result in a 70 percent increase. The other problem with task-specific productivity improvements is whether they impact project success. The goal of deploying machine learning software should be to increase the project success rate. Finding a more efficient way to allocate resources might save project costs, but does it significantly increase the probability of project success?

Some published articles proclaim that AI will automate a significant amount of a project manager's tasks (Gartner 2019). That means software would take almost everything that a project manager does now and turn it into a routine process that is repeated over and over again. Does a project manager really have that many repetitive tasks? The value of a project manager is to make good project decisions. AI software can be used to help the project manager make better decisions. The work of a project manager needs to change as routine administrative tasks are automated. AI is a disruptive technology that needs to be used to dramatically improve project performance. Automating existing administrative tasks only enhances productivity.

It is disturbing that many projects are constantly late and over budget. AI offers the potential to provide significant gains in productivity as long as project stakeholders are willing to adopt it. Although some excellent AI software helps automate project activities, doing so can take emphasis away from the actual value of AI, which is to dramatically improve the project methodology. Significant change is needed to consistently deliver projects on time and on or under budget. There is no reason to be afraid of incurring worse results since the risk of implementing AI software for project managers is no greater than any other technology, while the value can be significant. Implementing AI by automating smaller pieces of the process may be considered prudent, yet this may result in missing the most important gain, which is changing the project methodology. While productivity improvements deliver immediate and visible benefits, decision-making has the most significant impact on project results.

## QUESTIONS

### Review questions

1. What is the advantage of automating project management tasks?

2. What factors can be included when creating a business case for implementing AI technology in project management?

3. Why should project managers be concerned about taking an overall perspective of the project instead of taking advantage of productivity improvements in one specific area?

### Discussion questions

1. What are the obstacles to automating all project management functions?

2. Which approach is more beneficial: using AI to resolve a specific project problem or using AI to revise the process methodology?

## REFERENCES

DeSouza, J. and Meharwade, R. (2018). Individuals and interactions over processes and tools, can Agile be disrupted by artificial intelligence? Agile Alliance. Retrieved Dec 23, 2023. *https://www.agilealliance.org/resources/experience-reports/individuals-and-interactions-over-processes-and-tools/*

Gartner (2019). Gartner says 80 percent of today's project management tasks will be eliminated by 2030 as artificial intelligence takes over, *Gartner*. Retrieved Dec 23, 2023. *https://www.gartner.com/en/newsroom/press-releases/2019-03-20-gartner-says-80-percent-of-today-s-project-management*

Prieto SA, Mengiste ET, and García de Soto B. (2023). Investigating the Use of ChatGPT for the Scheduling of Construction Projects. *Buildings.* 13(4):857. *https://doi.org/10.3390/buildings13040857*

PART II

# *THE IMPORTANCE OF DATA*

A I software requires data to perform analysis and deliver results. *Big data* describes large, complex, and diverse datasets used for machine learning. For the analysis of medical conditions, a large volume of data is essential for accurate results. In business and project management, accurate results can be produced with a smaller amount of data. Data is critical and must be relevant to the project issue being addressed. Chapter 5 reviews data issues, focusing on providing project practitioners with an understanding of data as input for a machine learning algorithm. Project practitioners can make a valuable contribution to AI success by properly managing data requirements. Chapter 6 is about accessing and using the data. Data mining and predictive analytics are opportunities to gain insight from existing project data.

Organizations need to define a data strategy for project data. The information technology (IT) staff and project managers must work together to initiate and manage this strategy. For large project-based organizations, there needs to be an IT infrastructure that manages both data and AI software, and this typically includes decisions about using local servers or accessing the cloud, data architecture, data collection policies, and more. For smaller and medium-sized organizations, the problem is finding sufficient project data to train algorithms to produce results for their specific project. Using AI software is a valuable opportunity for project management. However, the process starts with being able to feed the software with data, and that may require a significant amount of work before the organization is ready.

# CHAPTER 5

# *PROVIDING GOOD PROJECT DATA*

D ata "feeds" all software algorithms. The importance of data cannot be underestimated, and if data is managed properly, the machine learning results provide enormous value to the organization and each project. One characteristic of data is that it is objective and not judgemental. A self driving car does not evaluate a person's character before it stops and lets them pass in front of the vehicle. Quality data is needed in the proper format and accessible for a machine learning algorithm to function properly. While this may seem like an overwhelming task, an advantage is that there is no need to evaluate the significance of each data field because that is what the machine learning algorithm does (as long as the data is related to project management).

A data strategy defines the process for capturing and storing project data. Providing input to a machine learning algorithm includes data availability, formatting, and overcoming the difficulties encountered with data. The strategy also needs to offer guidance on how to prepare for and manage the data that is required to feed AI software.

AI software works best with *structured data*, which is data that has been categorized, properly formatted, and made searchable. Data is the "backbone" of any AI system. For AI systems, the old expression "garbage in equals garbage out," as visualized in Figure 5.1, certainly applies. Organizations that utilize incorrect and poor-quality data will have poor or useless results.

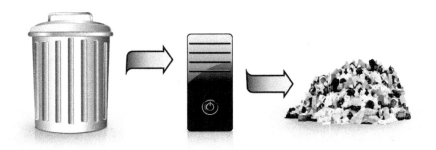

**FIGURE 5.1** How computers handle bad data

AI software results are certainly affected by the quality and quantity of data. However, a minimum number of datasets is required for the machine learning algorithms to be trained sufficiently and deliver a usable result. Organizations and project managers must understand the data preparation requirements for adopting AI-based functionality.

## MANAGING POOR DATA QUALITY ("GARBAGE IN")

Data is required to train an algorithm, and there are significant problems with data when implementing machine learning software. First, the data is typically not "clean," as demonstrated in Table 5.1. This table shows possible data issues that must be "cleaned" before the data can be used. The data fields can contain typos or improperly capitalized words. Field formats vary across databases and even within the same database. For example, a date field can be "dd/mm/yy," "mm/dd/yy," "mm/week," or "yyyy/mm/dd." There can be two data fields that have the same meaning and one data field that has two meanings. In one project, there was a data field for a pet owner's name, yet it could occasionally contain three names. (When this was questioned, the response was that everyone named considered themselves owners of the friendly pet.) There is usually a column of data with a single data field that is supposed to have a numeric value but is blank. Without specific directions, AI-based software cannot handle blank data fields. When encountering a blank data field, the software may describe the value as "NaN," which means "Not a Number." This results in an error unless steps are taken to prevent or remediate it. Should the programmer use an average of the numbers across the field, the median value, or a zero? There are many issues with data that must be resolved.

*TABLE 5.1* Examples of common data problems

| Problem | Example |
| --- | --- |
| Data entry errors | Project A |
| | Project a |
| Data meaning | Location |
| Raw data and derived data | Raw: 4, 10, 22 |
| | Derived: Average 12 |
| Format issues | dd/mm/yy |
| | mm/dd/yy |
| | yy/mm/dd |
| Blank data fields | 3, 0, 5, , 6, 12, 8 |
| Data elements per field | Owner name: Marie |
| | Owner name: Sam, Ajay, Devon |
| Duplicate data | Product certified Jun 23 |
| | Product certified June 23 |

Unfortunately, corrupt data can exist in a database and not cause any serious problems. Usually, it is only when an administrator encounters corrupt or bad data that a correction is made. When the data needs to be migrated to a new system, data issues can no longer be hidden, and work is required to discover and correct the problems. Another situation is if the existing database is accessed and used by another system, which causes issues in the other system. There is usually no incentive to clean data unless there is a pressing need, such as new technology or an upgrade to a new system. A business case can be made for upgrading software that uses a database, but it needs to include the cost and effort to clean the existing data. If not, then who is going to pay for the work? The effort needs to be sized and evaluated. Once funding is available, there are ways to get the work done. Some contractors and consulting businesses help with data migration by using software to validate the data and find anomalies. Then, the business must work to fix the anomalies, which can be very time-consuming. Some organizations hire a data architect, and part of that work is defining nomenclature or standards for critical data. Once data standards are determined and implemented, a validation process ensures remediation is complete. Following that, a process is initiated to maintain clean data. This is a better strategy than having none. However, the volume of stored data at some organizations means that they only define a set of critical data as part of the effort.

How does this apply to AI software? In a practical sense, the project manager needs to ensure historical project data is in a standard format and that there is consistency in capturing and storing the data. AI technology will become pervasive in organizations, and as time passes, an urgency to implement AI software will be necessary to remain competitive or survive as an organization. In that situation, a valid business case for work to clean and structure the data should be created because, without valid data, machine learning cannot produce accurate results. For the Agile methodology, data standards are also necessary because the shorter life cycle of sprints makes it more immediately worthwhile. Agile project sprints use recent or streaming data for machine learning algorithms to help the project maintain the expected performance.

## DATA VOLUME

A significant concern for organizations is the amount of data required. The data needs of organizations will vary from one situation to the next. Data scientists and machine learning specialists have not determined the exact amount of data required for every circumstance. For a medical diagnosis, a significant amount of historical data is needed. For a self driving car, large amounts of live-streaming data are required. For business models, somewhat less data is required, and there is machine learning software where as few as thirty project datasets are sufficient to produce accurate results.

In most, but not all situations, more data results in more accurate outcomes for prediction and classification. For large organizations, this may not be an issue. For example, a government will likely have considerable amounts of project data and project results and capture and store the data containing more project attributes. Smaller organizations may not have adequate data resources to use AI software. For example, there are many small organizations and associations that only implement a project every 8 to 10 years. They would not have the data required to successfully implement an AI solution. If they do need to use AI, they need to collaborate. In other words, there needs to be a project management database repository where small or medium-sized organizations share their data. Collaboration on data sharing helps take advantage of the advanced technology available to larger organizations.

An alternative is to use machine software that is already trained. While this may seem worthwhile, the results could be terrible. Imagine implementing a project to install a new email system based on machine learning software trained using construction project data. This could occur when a smaller organization contracts the project implementation to a solution provider. In this situation, the project sponsor must ensure that the contractor has access to AI software and a database that is effective for their project and their organization. Another possibility is to use open-source data. As momentum grows for increased AI usage in project management, groups are determined to accelerate project success by sharing data. If not addressed, the issue of data availability between larger and smaller entities will create a dichotomy. Larger organizations taking advantage of AI will become more successful, while smaller organizations fall behind.

## DATA SIGNIFICANCE

One of the problems with developing an AI capability for project management is the diversity of the types of projects. For example, there are construction projects, software development projects, and projects to change business processes. While the overriding principles of project management are the same, projects in different functional areas offer a unique challenge for AI. Machine learning requires data to train the algorithm which is usually project historical data including lessons learned. However, the lessons learned from a completed construction project may not be useful for a project with the goal of deploying software. While some commonality exists, it is more likely that an appropriate dataset from each project knowledge area is required.

The value of project management process knowledge is being able to apply a set of principles to any project. Although the principles are important, AI requires more specific details that allow an algorithm to consider relevant data to predict results and ultimately make an optimal decision for the project. Given this situation, the availability of good project data might be as valuable as the ability to create an algorithm that can take advantage of the data. How does an organization collect and store project data? In one project management survey, 75 percent of respondents claimed that their organization retains almost all project documents, including the budget and schedule documents. In addition, 40 percent claimed that their project documents were kept forever, while 50 percent retained them for four to ten years (Boudreau 2023).

Developing and using any AI software begins with data, which is the first significant issue. Data scientists managing big data, which are datasets too large to handle with traditional software, spend 60 to 80 percent of their time for an initial implementation on data cleaning tasks. This includes detecting bad data, removing or correcting data, and modifying data. If a business subjects its critical business data to data standards and adheres to those standards, there is evidence of a good data strategy. With very large datasets, the lack of clean data means that most data fields do not move easily into an array for further analysis. The issues range from simple items, such as having a data field with data in different formats, to more complicated items, such as detecting valid or invalid data in a field. Implementing AI to improve project performance is dependent on clean and manageable data. Organizations must understand this concept to take advantage of AI software. If they are not ready for the challenges associated with data, they will incur a cost for preparing and maintaining structured project data. The lack of proper data management will likely delay the benefits of utilizing AI technology and force organizations to seek incremental improvements instead of a significant advantage.

Let's consider an example. A database has over a million pieces of data divided into various categories. It is impossible for the human brain alone to discover similarities or dependencies in this amount of data. A machine learning program using different classifiers is capable of doing this. This type of software is extremely valuable for challenging tasks, such as the interpretation and diagnosis of MRI brain scans or lung x-rays in children because the level of accuracy is much higher than that of a skilled technician. Fortunately, for project management, millions of datasets are not required. With a sound data strategy and proper data management, far less data still provides usable results.

Improving the accuracy of input data can also be applied to project management. Specifically, how does a project manager accurately diagnose a serious project issue and make the best decision to resolve the issue? An optimal solution involves three types of data: the past, the present, and the future.

1. *The past.* AI programs that rely on machine learning use historical information for training and then make a prediction for a new set of data. For project management, the software program will look for similarities based on historical information from previous projects. One critical document is an issues log or problem register that contains the issues, decision, and resulting outcome. What occurred, and was there a successful resolution? Organizations store project data but fail to obtain value. Project data is like a gold coin stored away in a dark cupboard. Historical information has value and needs to be used to improve project performance.

2. *The present.* AI software for project management needs to include the current project status and project environment. These are important factors in determining the best solution to an issue or problem. Project documents capture project events and results, typically status reports or dashboard metrics. Current project data includes basic information such as budget, schedule, change orders, risks, and earned value management (EVM) metrics. The project environment includes internal factors, such as the organization's policies and procedures, and external factors, such as interest rates for loans, contractor prices, inflation, and resource availability. Factors in the current project environment are required to evaluate the probability of success for various solutions or actions derived by AI software.

3. *The future.* The final category extends the ability of an artificial intelligence program into a different area, which is metrics about the future. What is likely to happen in the next few years or for the remaining duration of the project? This may seem like speculation, but both the internal and external environments exhibit trends that can be captured and used to assist in finding the best decision for project issues. Let's consider the example of interest rates. In a

climate where interest rates are low, and inflation is beginning to climb, a rise in rates in the future can be expected. Of course, the central bank for a country also issues statements that they expect to raise or lower rates in the future, so there is not much speculation at all. Trends such as the expected growth rates and resource availability are widely available in publications such as the *Economist* or published by a government organization. Capturing exact data for future events may not always be possible, but the data can be expected to fall within a specific range.

A project's internal environment may reveal a trend due to the inability to achieve budget targets and result in a forecast of the estimate at completion (EAC) based on the cost performance index (CPI) run rate. While some results, such as a sporting event, may be unpredictable, there are many future metrics that easily fall within a limited set of parameters. These can be similar to predicting the path of an iceberg. The iceberg may move slightly in one direction or another, but the direction is obvious. Gathering all these factors enhances an AI software's ability to consider data and make accurate assessments and predictions for project decisions. A machine learning program that considers the past, present, and future is a powerful tool for determining the best outcome to solve project issues.

A *corpus* is a body or work, usually a large and structured body of texts. For example, a movie review database with ratings or an opinion database containing English words categorized as expressing positive or negative sentiment. A challenge of project management is that words can often have a different meaning in the context of a project than in general usage. For example, if a chatbot such as Siri or Alexa is asked about a "schedule," it assumes the request is for a personal calendar of appointments. In project management, a "schedule" is a list of tasks in the project that are sequenced based on dependencies. To accomplish some natural language processing, there needs to be a way to interpret project management language properly.

There also needs to be a logic resource to support proper decision-making. For example, the *Project Management Body of Knowledge* (PMBOK) has a list of techniques used to determine actions to find the best outcome. Various bodies of knowledge used in project management provide similar or even better results. When using a virtual assistant such as Alexa, Siri, or Google Assistant and asking about a change control process for a project, the answer requires knowledge about how to manage a project's scope. Similarly, asking if a specific task can be delayed to a different week or if resources can be shifted without a negative impact on the scheduled end date requires knowledge of the logic regarding a critical path. A proper and logical sequence allows a project manager to answer these questions easily, but a knowledgeable reference with project management logic is required in addition to the data.

A project status consists of a variety of metrics. Is the project on schedule? Is the budget overspent? This may include earned value management metrics. An AI program accesses and applies these metrics to assess the current project status. In addition, future project metrics are calculated, such as "Will the project end date be on schedule?" This is different from whether the project is on schedule at this moment in time. Attempting to predict if the project will finish on or under budget requires a different approach from evaluating the current status. The logic sources for a project provide input for calculating these values if they are not already part of routine project metrics that are collected and accessible to the machine learning algorithm.

Gathering and maintaining data involve significant amounts of work. Part of a project data strategy is determining what data needs to be retained and what data will be used or discarded. In a machine learning program, data can be used to train the algorithm and is no longer required unless used for updates, as in reinforcement learning. Similarly, there may be an opportunity to use streaming data to train a model rather than capturing and storing it.

## QUESTIONS

### Review questions

1. How does input data and the volume of data affect results?

2. What types of data are available in managing projects?

**Discussion questions**

1. How can a project manager avoid the situation of "garbage in" for project data?

2. How does the diversity of project types have an impact on project data collection?

## REFERENCES

Boudreau, P. (2023). [Unpublished raw data regarding project data retention in organizations] *https://www.pmi.org/search#q=polls%20data%20retention&sort=relevancy*

## CASE STUDY: INSUFFICIENT DATA

A large pharmaceutical company initiates several projects to improve the IT services in the organization. The projects consistently run over schedule, so the organization adds Agile processes. The projects continue to be delivered late. The company contacts a consultant to evaluate an AI solution to forecast a more accurate project schedule end date.

The company delivers its project data in a spreadsheet. There are 35 projects, with 15 characteristics from each project. When examined, the consultant identifies several duplicate data fields, some data fields with inconsistent formats, and one field with data from an external source. There are also two data fields that contain unusable data, such as a sequential change order number. In total, there are only three usable data fields for AI analysis.

1. How much data is required to perform the analysis?

2. What feedback should the consultant provide to the company?

3. How can the data collection process be improved?

# 6

# *ACQUIRING AND USING DATA*

A project management plan typically consists of various documents, such as the project scope statement, a schedule, a resource allocation plan, a risk register, and other plans. How does AI software access these documents? The easiest method is to ensure they are stored in a common repository (Barcaui and Monat 2024; Paver 2024). Each past project is uniquely categorized, so these documents can be considered a dataset. Text documents can be read using NLP, and the characteristics can be extracted to a numerical format. Spreadsheets can be imported into a DataFrame in Python and used by the algorithm. The variety of formats, such as text documents, PDFs, spreadsheets, and presentation formats, can make accessing the data challenging. A high level of effort is required to access, read, and interpret all these project documents, which explains why AI software development companies need to hire so many NLP specialists.

Some organizations have vast amounts of stored project data, which could be extremely useful for training a machine learning algorithm. Classification is a typical machine learning outcome, and one application for project management is to evaluate if a risk is likely to occur on a project. An added benefit can be that the machine learning software reads that data and becomes trained but does not need to retain any data as part of the training. This is the way that some Web sites work. They do not capture the keystrokes that are attached to a user. Instead, they use the keystrokes to train the model with no requirement to keep the data, resulting in no personal privacy issues for the user. Other Web sites capture user data to target users for specific recommendations. The value of machine learning is that it is unbiased in determining the correlations. The algorithm may not need to retain information and can be an anonymous reader. In other words, a top-secret clearance might be required to view data in a document, but because the machine learning software does not retain any data, the same classification level may not be necessary. The machine learning software learns from the data and does not remember any of the data. This is useful for military, defense, or tax information, where there is a risk of having a person review the documents and discover names or improperly followed processes. Machine learning does not judge the sources of data or the data content. It uses the data to train itself to make the next project successful.

Organizations such as governments tend to have large quantities of data and are a good target for data analytics. The goal is to increase project success rates. To help projects be more successful, the results need to reveal what aspects of past projects created or caused project problems that led to an unsuccessful outcome. Minor improvements may be discovered via data mining, but the objective is to find a significant cause of project delays and budget overruns. Higher success rates start by ensuring that a project has comprehensive project management plans and a proper strategy that will result in a successful project after uncovering the causes using predictive analytics. Based on the data, adjustments can be made to future projects to avoid similar problems, assuming the organization is willing and able to make changes to the project methodology. The next step is to develop and implement AI software that can be trained to ensure that the project starts well and remains on track to achieve the project outcome.

## DATA MINING

*Data mining* involves searching for patterns and correlations in data, but it is not a replacement for machine learning. Data mining is used to analyze large databases to discover statistical patterns and provide insights to create a higher probability of project success (Vandersluis 2013). For an organization with a significant amount of stored project data, data mining software that classifies the data or finds anomalies is an excellent opportunity to extract value. The objective is to determine what makes a project successful in this type of organization. An investigation can reveal if there are common factors that are detrimental to the projects, especially when people cannot determine what happened. In data mining, detecting an anomaly in the data is the identification of an outlier that may be interesting and require further investigation. For example, in project management, it could answer why the project was so late compared to the normal distribution of the statistical results.

## HOW TO PREPARE THE DATA

There are activities that a project manager or PMO can undertake to prepare for AI. Data is important, and the organization must create and implement a data strategy. The best course of action is to ensure that there is a repository for data that is already being captured. In most projects, this includes the scope statement, budget, schedule, change orders, risks, and a list of issues or problems that typically had to be resolved due to a status meeting.

The scope statement describes the project's detail or depth of complexity. Some scope statements are small, while others are hundreds of pages. Change requests are tracked by status in a review and acceptance process. Some are approved, becoming a change order, and some are rejected or deferred. It is important to capture the change order details, as this may indicate a deficiency in the original scope or it may indicate scope creep.

Status documents need to provide a usable level of detail. A statement that "resources are inadequate" is not as helpful as documenting the gap, such as the true level of resources required and any other considerations, such as training or availability. A structured "lessons learned" document can be used as input for several purposes. While documents such as the scope statement may be acceptable in their current form, the lessons learned for complex projects require a structured format and details that may not be typically captured. For example, a typical "lessons learned" issue results in an action item to resolve the issue for future projects. This might be an update to an organization's policy or a new communication requirement. Additional data should be captured if the action item achieved the desired result or if the same issue returns in other projects. A new perspective on lessons learned is to use it to capture data at designated points during project implementation. Rather than wait until the entire project is complete, a process is added to identify issues and actions that are useful for a machine learning algorithm. This process also ensures that the data required for AI software is captured. As projects progress and AI software provides more value, organizations identify and capture more specific data for machine learning algorithms. A continuous learning approach to understanding data extracts more value from AI solutions and improves project performance.

A project status meeting can uncover various issues or problems that must be resolved. Two simple examples are a training course that does not include an essential requirement or a team member not being available at a required time. An action item is taken with a due date and an assigned person responsible. The issues log needs to capture if the action is successful. The issues log is important because it is a snapshot of the project's progress toward the due dates. Most project data will be historical data, and while the issues data is also historical, it has a current aspect that makes it more valuable.

**TABLE 6.1** Typical sample issues report

| | Issue | Description | Assigned | Due Date | Resolution |
|---|---|---|---|---|---|
| 1 | Training Course Gap | The training course does not include data maintenance | Person A | 23 March | Renegotiated with a contractor to add the content |
| 2 | Resource Shortage | The technical expert is unavailable for the next 2 weeks | Person B | 20 May | Acquired a replacement on loan from another project |

**TABLE 6.2** Typical sample issues report: Additional fields for machine learning

| Issue | Resolution | Due Date | Budget Impact | Schedule Impact |
|---|---|---|---|---|
| 1 Training Course Gap | Renegotiated with a contractor to include the dditional content | 23 March | $20,000 | 2 days |
| 2 Resource Shortage | Acquired a replacement on loan from another project | 20 May | None | 5 days |

Deploying a successful machine learning algorithm requires the correct data, not just any data. Project managers can work with IT staff to ensure the data being used is a good fit for the model. This is not meant to restrict what the machine learning software should access because that might make it less accurate. The data must fit within the project parameters for the software being used.

Someone in the organization needs to take responsibility for data management for projects. This includes creating or maintaining a repository that can be accessed by various AI software algorithms and still retain security around personal or proprietary data. The following are important aspects of being able to use project management data.

1. *Structure the data.* There are relatively simple changes that can be performed to make the data more usable. For example, a status report can be structured so that the type of issue is consistently identified. It may be helpful to create specific categories and use them across all documents. A scope issue should be related to a particular section in the scope statement document. The same is true for the risk register. The risks should be linked to activities that relate to the project plan and in the scope statement. This approach seems like it will result in more work, but in reality, it is simply being better organized, and it helps everyone understand the interconnections in the project.

   For the overall project, a judgment on success needs to be defined. What makes this project successful from a project point of view? Did it meet the requirements for budget and schedule? This helps by creating a label for the project, which is useful for supervised learning. One of the distinctions that needs to be made is whether the project met the customer's expectations. That is important but not necessarily the goal of AI software. AI software increases the probability of the project process. In many cases, that will result in both project success and a customer recognition of success. There may be circumstances where the project is completed, and the project outcome is no longer aligned or effective for the customer's organization. It may be possible for AI software to monitor and correlate data from the external environment to include this as a probability factor for meeting customer expectations.

2. *Store the project data.* Each completed project and all completed documents must be stored in an accessible repository. Project closure is normally the process where this type of work occurs. The closing stage of a project also tends to be the stage where

everyone is happy that the project is complete and ready to move on to the next project. Time pressures or other distractions may prevent effective work. Project closure can be tedious administrative work, but there must be a process to ensure proper project data retention.

3. *Maintain data integrity.* Once project data is structured, it must be consistently formatted across all projects in the organization. This might be easy for some organizations but will be difficult for others. If a PMO exists, they can enforce a level of standards. Otherwise, each project manager must commit to maintaining data standards throughout the project.

There is open-source software, such as TensorFlow, that provides an easy way to load, manipulate, and feed data to a machine learning model. Preprocessing of input data can include normalizing a value, converting a string to an integer, and converting a floating-point number to an integer. Data management software can handle large volumes of data more efficiently. Hadoop is another type of open-source software, and it is used for distributed processing of large datasets across clusters of connected computer servers. It can scale up to thousands of machines and is currently one of the most widely used software solutions for managing, storing, and processing big data.

The advantage of AI software is that the number of documents, size, and complexity do not impede success. A disadvantage of current project documents is that to be successful, the documents may need to be connected. This may involve including tags to indicate linkages across all documents instead of considering them independent documents that contain abstract or generic references to other aspects of the project. NLP software may be unable to make the connection that a specific risk is linked to several other tasks. It might not even be known that a quality measurement is linked to a project's deliverable, which is defined in the scope document. If the links are apparent, they will be interpreted properly by generative AI software. Projects frequently have complex interconnections where links are less obvious, and making sure they are known helps AI software make good decisions.

*TABLE 6.3* Sample project activity list

| Act ID | Activity |
| --- | --- |
| 1 | Define the process |
| 2 | Create a data map |
| 3 | Create test cases |
| 4 | Configure the processes |
| 5 | Perform user reviews |
| 6 | Perform Configuration |

*TABLE 6.4* Sample project risk list

| Description | Owner | Response Strategy | Activity ID Link |
| --- | --- | --- | --- |
| Risk 1 | Risk Owner A | Response strategy 1 | 3, 4 |
| Risk 2 | Risk Owner B` | Response strategy 2 | 4 |

A machine learning algorithm might be able to learn the linkages from historical data using generative AI, but only where the events illustrate that the actual linkages occurred. The links in Table 6.4 demonstrate how it can be done and are not representative of all linkages in a project. Many others, such as resources and quality requirements, may not be linked directly to a specific activity. The interconnections using links in the data are an important mechanism for AI software to successfully crawl through project data and extrapolate issues that require adjustments to optimize the project's performance.

In project management, project documents are not clean and easy to read. It is fairly straightforward to use NLP to read a document if it is in Word or PDF. Then, the machine learning software uses logic to perform classification or prediction. It is more complicated to read a project schedule, though. Additional logic is required to understand the meaning of a critical path and be able to interpret the sequence and dependencies. For example, consider whether the software can invoke the critical path chart view and look for the red line that indicates critical path activities. Once the complexity of access and interpretation is solved, float and free float need to be calculated, and then resource loading needs to be reviewed.

Implementing AI to interpret a project schedule requires a knowledgeable project manager to understand the data and use an overlay of machine learning to identify errors and provide predictions. To have a complete picture of the project, other factors that interact with the schedule, such as risk and quality, must also be considered. The complexity of reading a schedule includes understanding the task dependencies and critical path, possibly earned value management metrics, and how the schedule interacts with the aspects of the project. AI software is changing how the critical path concept is applied, but it begins by being able to access and interpret the data (Quong 2023).

## DATA MANAGEMENT TERMS AND ACTIONS

*Data wrangling* is a term that refers to the work of analyzing and preparing raw data into a format or structure that can be used by machine learning software. Roughly 60 to 80 percent of the time spent for an initial AI deployment is preparing the data.

*Categorical data* is data that is not numerical, such as a color or location. In risk management, the risks might be rated as high, medium, or low. To convert this data into numerical values, a technique known as one-hot encoding, as shown in Table 6.5, is applied for a machine learning algorithm using binary regression analysis.

**TABLE 6.5** Using one-hot encoding for categorical data

| | | | |
|---|---|---|---|
| High | 0 | 0 | 1 |
| Medium | 0 | 1 | 0 |
| Low | 1 | 0 | 0 |

*Feature engineering* is the process of selecting and manipulating data to allow a machine learning algorithm to produce acceptable results. Consider a situation where there are three data fields that have a similar meaning. A decision is made to select one and eliminate the others. Another option is to take an average of the values and turn this into derived data. There may be insufficient data, and additional project characteristics are needed to improve the analysis.

It may be possible to train the algorithm with the data as it is reported or immediately after the project has ended, which alleviates the need to store data. Research has been performed on how machine learning software can take streaming data as input and process that into a model that can produce results (Plamendon 2018). This poses the question whether the data needs to be stored or if it is sufficient to feed the data directly to machine learning software to provide what can be called *real time training*.

From an IT perspective, a large organization needs a plan for the objective of machine learning software and have sufficient capacity and flexibility to fit into the organization's current data strategy. Data standards need to be determined (unless they are already in place) and adherence is being met. With more than one AI software program, there may be a requirement for an infrastructure design. As each new software solution becomes available, the data approach needs to be comprehensive and not short-sighted or fragmented. Also, the data flow needs to be communicated and adhered to so that data is available without obstacles or restrictions. Ideally, all the project documents are included in a common repository. In the design of the system, there may be a need to evaluate and determine if it is appropriate to use a data platform capable of increasing data storage reliably and cost-effectively. There also needs to be consideration of an on-premises or cloud solution. There are many factors to consider in this decision, which will most likely be decided based on the organization's data strategy.

The challenge with introducing new technology in projects is that every project is unique. All projects follow some standard basic processes and require the creation of project documents. Generative AI is being used to search for anomalies across project documents to verify the project plan's completeness, accuracy, and coherence. Machine learning uses historical data from similar projects to predict where the project will likely have problems and why the problems are likely to occur, and it describes the ensuing impact on the project scope, budget, and schedule. AI can serve as a project management aid that performs analysis with results that quickly increase project success rates.

Machine learning is a valuable technology but only one piece of the system. A structured and extensive database provides input, and project managers interpret and take action on the results. There needs to be a data collection stage and a data verification process that ensures the data is structured and usable. The features or critical elements used by the machine learning software are identified in the data. Once the machine learning results are produced, there may need to be further analysis, or at least a procedure should be in place regarding how the results will be used and what actions will be taken.

Lack of data is a serious issue when building predictive models for project management. Insufficient data in a machine learning model causes a problem known as *underfitting.* This problem occurs when there is not enough data for an algorithm to properly learn the correlations and create an accurate model, which results in inaccurate predictions. Figure 6.1 shows insufficient data points to create a valid correlation.

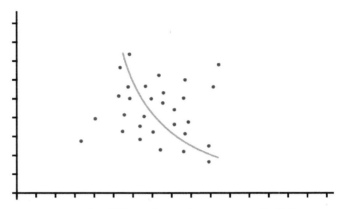

*FIGURE 6.1* Insufficient data points cause underfitting.

Another challenge is that a model may be too simple; the actual model might require a more complex algorithm. A successful model should consist of more than historical data and include current project data or any results that provide feedback into the model that continuously improves the prediction's accuracy. *Overfitting* is creating a model using statistics that attempts to match the data too closely. In this situation, there are outliers that should be ignored, but the machine learning algorithm tries to include them as part of the model. The result is a model that may not predict future observations accurately. In Figure 6.2, the correlation line is too exact, which makes predictions less accurate.

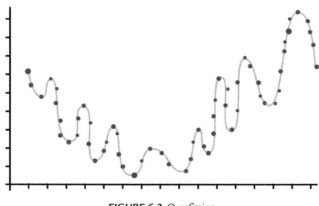

*FIGURE 6.2* Overfitting

Data scientists are in high demand to prepare and manage data, and they command a high level of compensation. Project managers are in an excellent position to perform this type of work. The project manager understands project terminology and can assess data fields to determine duplication or meaning. With some basic data management training, project managers can dramatically increase their value to the organization by taking on part of the role of a data scientist and providing input to machine learning algorithms.

## QUESTIONS

### Review questions

1. Explain the difference between data wrangling and feature engineering.

2. In what ways does the organization's size affect data collection?

3. How do organizations collect the "right" data instead of "any" data?

### Discussion questions

1. Does data mining help or hinder an organization that wants to implement AI solutions?

2. Can an organization collect too much data when deploying AI in project management?

3. Who should perform feature engineering, a data scientist or a project manager?

## REFERENCES

Barcaui, A. and Monat, A. (2024). The PM data repository, retrieved January 17, 2024, *https://www.pmdatarep.com/*

Paver, M. (2024). Join the construction data trust, Retrieved January 17, 2024, *https://www.srm.com/news-and-comment/ join-the-construction-data-trust/*

Plamendon A. (2018). Autonomous learning for autonomous systems, lecture, *Machine Learning and Artificial Intelligence Ottawa*, September 2018.

Quong, C. (2023). Case Studies at Octantai. *www.ocantai.com*

Vandersluis, C. (2013). Panning for gold by data-mining your project tracking data, *presented at PMI Global Congress 2013—North America, New Orleans, Project Management Institute, https://www. pmi.org/learning/library/project-data-mining-techniques-5854.*

# PART III

# AI SOLUTIONS FOR PROJECT PROBLEMS

This section challenges the concept of how projects are managed and presents how to use AI to change the project methodology. The purpose of applying AI to project management is to improve project performance. AI capabilities and how they can be used to improve project success rates are discussed. Some AI-based solutions will be disruptive and change how projects are managed, and some will provide significant efficiency improvements to one aspect of project management that needs it. It is common to read sensational headlines about the high amount of funding for AI development. Funding needs to be applied correctly to solve the most pressing problems, and very little of that will likely be applied directly to project management (Holst 2019). Another challenge regarding AI software is optimizing or getting the most value from the implemented AI solutions. Consider the analogy of Microsoft Word, where everyone uses, on average, about ten to twenty menu items, yet over a hundred are available. AI software for project management has common uses, but taking full advantage of the capability means being creative and finding extra features that increase project performance. Finding and taking advantage of a capability that is not obvious in a software application provides significant improvement beyond what is expected when the software is acquired. The examples in this section are also meant to improve the understanding of AI-based solutions. A number of concepts are used to solve project problems, but project managers must think beyond productivity gains. AI concepts offer flexibility, and project managers need to think about how AI can be applied to improve every area of managing a project.

Chapter 7 explains how machine learning addresses different project management areas. Supervised learning, unsupervised learning, and reinforcement learning are all valuable algorithms used for prediction and classification. Chapter 8 reviews natural language processing (NLP) and its many applications to project management. Because of virtual assistants and translation software, NLP tends to be more visible than machine learning, which is processing the data that provides direction for the NLP response. Generative AI is an example of combining machine learning and NLP to deliver results, as described in Chapter 9. This section concludes with an explanation of genetic algorithms in Chapter 10.

# CHAPTER 7

# PREDICTING PROJECT RESULTS USING MACHINE LEARNING ALGORITHMS AND SUPERVISED LEARNING TO PREDICT RESULTS

It would be amazing if project managers had access to software that could accurately predict the success of a project before it started. It would almost be like being at the end of a project and knowing all the issues and problems that developed. The purpose of prediction is to move that knowledge to the start of the project. The resources and energy saved by preventing a "doomed" project are valuable, but even more valuable is ensuring that every project begins with a high probability of success. This is one of the ways that AI software has an impact on project management processes. A project success prediction algorithm calculates the probability of success for a project before it begins based on an analysis of the project management information available for project implementation. AI prediction software is a program consisting of an algorithm that can use a neural network to correlate patterns in the data to create a supervised learning model. The data is provided from a series of historical projects, with a set of data captured for each project. The projects are labeled "success" or "failure" as defined by the user. The AI model is trained using historical data, analyzes the project planning documents for a newly proposed project, and calculates a probability of success based on the model created from the training data. The machine learning algorithm performs regression analysis to forecast the probability of project success based on various factors used as input to the algorithm. Why would anyone start implementing a project with a low probability of success? The capability of an AI-based prediction algorithm makes it a powerful aid for project managers, project sponsors, and the PMO.

## EXAMPLE: PREDICTION SOFTWARE

Prediction software consists of three components: the input data, software containing the machine learning algorithm, and output. The input data typically consists of several characteristics based on historical projects completed by an organization or within an industry. Each project is labeled as "successful" or "not successful." Success can be user-defined for an organization. For example, the definition can be delivering the project scope no more than five percent over budget or five percent late to the scheduled end date. The definition is flexible as long as it is consistently applied to each project in the dataset. The definition assumes that the quality requirements are defined in the scope document and that risk factors affect the budget or schedule. Since the projects have labeled datasets, the algorithm is trained using a supervised learning model. Alternative algorithm functions, such as support vector machines (SVMs) and random forest classifiers are possible, but a neural network produces the most consistent and accurate results (Thomas 2019). A typical output of a neural network used for project prediction is the probability of project success. The machine learning software correlates features in the datasets into a model that represents an image of success for a project. Unlike a traditional project methodology that postulates that every process must be included to be successful, the machine learning algorithm decides what *pattern* of features contributes the most to achieving the label. The output is a prediction of probability that is too complex for a project manager to determine from looking at the data.

How much data is required for prediction software to make accurate predictions? The answer can be determined by research and testing and will vary based on the type of organization or project. This is a problem that data scientists continue to work on. As noted in an earlier example, the medical field requires more data to increase the probability of an accurate diagnosis. In business, the requirement can be somewhat less (valid results can be obtained with 30 to 50 datasets). More datasets and a selection of relevant features are preferred. For different areas of project management, a limited number of datasets requires more testing and verification. There is likely a range of datasets that are adequate, and there is no exact amount. Some organizations consistently maintain a project database for current and historical projects that is extensive enough to use as input for machine learning software. Other organizations do not understand the value of project data as it relates to implementing projects. Developing a data strategy is a valuable plan for machine learning implementation. All organizational data is valuable, and increasing project success rates depends on capturing more data that helps improve the project methodology.

There are negative implications of having insufficient data and creating inaccurate models. As mentioned, training machine learning software with insufficient data causes underfitting, which decreases the accuracy of the prediction. Overfitting distorts the model by trying to fit in outliers. Both of these occurrences reduce the ability to make accurate predictions.

As prediction software becomes common in project management, the amount of data required to build an accurate model will be easier to determine. Models are created and then modified based on test data as practitioners become experienced in understanding how the model works. Any model used for accurate predictions still depends on the input data.

## PROJECT SCREENING AND SELECTION

The project screening process usually consists of criteria used to screen out unsuitable projects. For example, the financial benefit may be too low or the time period for implementation too long. The screening factors can be unique to an organization or standard across many projects. Calculating the probability of success for a project is an opportunity to add another standard factor for project screening. The project screening process normally looks like a funnel, as shown in Figure 7.1.

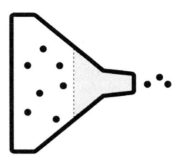

**FIGURE 7.1** Project screening process

Looking at this from a different perspective, the screening process provides threshold values for projects to receive further consideration in the process. The benefit of using prediction software at this stage is that all projects are evaluated to the same standard. If one project receives a 72 percent probability of success, and the second project receives a 95 percent probability of success, then one project has a clear advantage. The organization determines the acceptable probability level for the projects to move forward for further consideration.

The project selection process aims to select the best project from several alternatives. There are many factors to consider, such as the financial and strategic value of each project. Adding a metric such as the probability of success adds a layer of confidence that the objectives defined by the strategic and financial benefits are achievable. A weighted scoring model can include the probability of success in selecting the best project. The factor must also be reviewed as a stand-alone item subject to more scrutiny. Of course, customers or sponsors are likely to select a project with a success probability of 95 percent instead of a project with a success probability of 65 percent. What actions are required if a project with a 65 percent probability must be implemented? This project may be needed for legal, regulatory, or strategic reasons. When faced with a low probability of success, one possible action is for the project manager to gather the project team and rework the project implementation strategy. Project managers are planners and know that more work completed to create a successful plan normally means more straightforward implementation. Perhaps something is missing in the documentation, or the strategy is inadequate. Whatever the issue, the planning for this project needs to be improved to achieve a higher probability of success before the project begins. This is not simulation software, so the prediction will not automatically tell project managers what factors need to be improved. When seeing a poor probability of success, most project managers will likely quickly identify weak areas or areas where the project plan requires a better strategy. Using AI in the project screening and selection process is summarized in Table 7.1.

**TABLE 7.1** Using a project outcome success prediction in project initiation

| Process | Purpose | AI Prediction Software |
|---|---|---|
| Project Screening | Projects must meet a threshold or are eliminated | Include the success probability result as one of the screening criteria |
| Project Selection | The best projects are selected among alternatives that have passed the screening process | Include success probability as a factor for consideration. |
| Mandatory Project | The project must proceed due to legal, regulatory, or strategic reasons | Increase the probability of success by reviewing and upgrading the planning documents and implementation strategy |

## PREDICTIONS DURING PROJECT EXECUTION

While a probability of success before the project begins provides insight into the potential for project success, some enhancements make this type of software even more helpful, possibly invaluable. The prediction software is used as the project is underway to determine whether the probability of success is increasing or decreasing. This is incredibly valuable information. Let's consider a hypothetical video game called *Project Management*. In the game, the main character, a project manager, is at the start of a long hallway with doors on both sides. The project manager walks along the hallway and then places their hand on a doorknob on a door to the right. Before opening the door, the project manager runs the prediction software, which indicates that the project's probability of success has now dropped to 45 percent. The project manager ignores that door and rapidly walks further down the hallway, turning to a door on the left. The project manager places a hand on the doorknob but, before opening it, runs the prediction software. The result indicates that the project now has a 98 percent probability of success. In our hypothetical video game, the doors represent project decisions. The prediction algorithm inside the game helps the project manager make good decisions to increase and maintain a high probability of success for the project as it is being implemented.

The data requirements to maintain a successful project include typical project status metrics, including metrics related to scope, schedule, and budget. Earned value management metrics are especially useful. Additional value is offered by updating the factors on which the project was approved, such as the return on investment or payback period. Environmental factors can be collected, if appropriate. External factors may include the rate of inflation, bank lending rate, or the duration it takes to acquire resources. The data collected can also include future metrics such as the expected growth of the organization, expected price of commodities, and economic forecast data. Of course, the cost or inability to collect the data is challenging for some organizations. Once the factors are determined, AI software analyzes the trends as either helpful to the project, meaning an increased probability of success, or detrimental to the project, meaning a decreased probability of success. In addition, specific project decisions are evaluated to determine whether they improve the probability of a successful result. There are many other ways to use prediction software. The advantage of understanding and adopting AI software is that it is capable of delivering predictions in many project areas. AI deciphers data in a unique, complex way, providing an advantage in using this technology to complete more projects successfully.

Predictions are not limited to project success. There are many potential areas in which to make predictions, such as the following:

- Agile sprint prediction: Predict the results of a sprint.

- risk probability: Predict if a risk will occur and if it will cause an impact on project success.

- stakeholder management influence: Predict whether stakeholders will have a positive or negative impact on the project. Determine if stakeholder behavior is a risk to project performance.

- basic Agile process success: Predict if the Agile process will deliver the expected results.

- resource issues: Predict if resource issues will result in project delays.

- schedule issues: Predict if issues for critical path and non-critical path activities will threaten the project end date.

- budget issues: Predict if the budget is accurate. Predict budget deterioration as the project progresses.

- communication issues: Determine if communication issues will cause a negative impact on project performance.

- portfolio interactions: Predict if other projects will negatively influence project results.

- quality issues: Predict if quality issues will occur. Determine if poor quality will result in project failure.

- procurement issues: Predict the vendor most likely to succeed.

- vendor execution: Predict if vendor performance will have a negative impact on project results.

Each supervised learning template captures characteristics or *features* (as they are known in the machine learning terms). The definition for the features can be flexible as long as the definition is applied consistently across all datasets. The number of features is also flexible, although using an unreasonably high number of features may not add value to the calculations.

## USING PREDICTION SOFTWARE IN A GATING PROCESS

Some organizations use a *gate process* to divide projects into distinct phases or stages. The gates are clearly defined milestones achieved when all the tasks required by each milestone are complete. Examples of three stages in a gate process are design, test, and deployment. The gate itself also becomes a review and decision point in the project. This allows an organization to carefully review the project's progress and accomplishments. In addition, a gate normally has a checklist that must be completed to allow the project to proceed to the next stage. It is a control point for several concerns, such as funding, quality, risk, and scheduling. Prediction software helps organizations manage the gating process for projects.

There can be a problem when a project arrives at a gate, passes the checklist, and fails during the next stage. Prediction software can mitigate this challenge in several ways. First, it is possible that the checklist does not contain all the data elements necessary for the project to complete the next stage successfully. After all, it usually consists of completed tasks. AI can determine if the risk increased since the start of the project or if anomalies might have occurred. Prediction software can analyze historical data from projects and make a judgment as to the probability of passing the next gate. The second way prediction software can be used in this situation is to consider the factors the project will manage in the next stage and correlate that data into a higher or lower probability of success if the project proceeds. This is also the point where modifications can be made to the project plan to increase the probability of success for the project.

*TABLE 7.2* Using prediction in a gate process

| Process | Purpose | AI Prediction Software Usage |
|---|---|---|
| Phase or Stage Gate | Complete a checklist and decide to allow the project to continue | Consider historical data to predict the probability of success. Use current metrics and environmental data up to the next gate to predict the probability of success |

As shown in Table 7.2, the gating process provides an opportunity to capture project data vital to using AI-based software to manage projects. Organizations can use this step to include all the data requirements necessary in a checklist to ensure machine learning algorithms have up-to-date and relevant data to make future project decisions. Predictions reflect the culture and success of the organization. AI software does not resolve poorly designed and poorly executed projects. It only confirms that they will fail. An organization with a good structure and clear project processes that is consistently capturing project data will likely be more successful in adopting and using prediction software.

One of the problems in utilizing prediction software is the availability of data. Businesses typically will not readily provide data for projects that have not been successfully completed. In addition, many organizations consider their project data to be proprietary, and perhaps some may even consider their project implementation processes a critical success factor. (Of course, that assumes that they are consistently successful with project implementation, something rare in most organizations.) Machine learning software for project management can suffer from a lack of data, resulting in underfitting. In this scenario, the algorithm does not have enough data to properly learn correlations and subsequently make accurate predictions. The initial model that was developed may be too simple, and the company may require the creation of a more complex algorithm. A genuinely successful model should consist of historical data, current project data, and any results that can improve prediction accuracy. In addition, there will be external factors that are difficult to quantify, such as the hiring of contractors or acquiring a vendor to deliver the project. The ability and adequacy of contractors can be considered a risk and added to the risk factors included in the data provided to the prediction algorithm. In issuing a request for proposal (RFP), one of the criteria can be for the vendor to include prediction results based on their plan. There are no easy solutions to external factors and the lack of data, especially if an organization is at the earlier stages of AI implementation for project management. It is too presumptuous to determine whether projects need to be organized by common factors such as function or objective rather than having a single algorithm that fits all projects. Will there be a need to build AI models that are only effective with certain types of projects, such as construction, software implementation, or business process redesign projects? General project prediction software is unlikely to determine accurate results for all projects. The algorithm may be the same, but at the very least, the input data needs to be appropriate for each project type.

## AN EXAMPLE OF DEVELOPING PREDICTION SOFTWARE

The following example is based on developing a supervised learning algorithm for project management. The software in this example consists of a three-layer neural network, as shown in Figure 7.2.

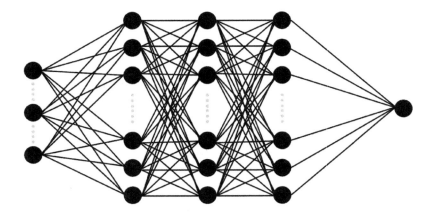

*FIGURE 7.2* A graphical representation of a three-layer neural network

In Figure 7.2, the column on the left represents the input layer. In this example, the input contains 50 datasets (projects) of 87 features plus a column that labels each dataset as "successful." This schematic represents supervised learning. The three columns in the middle perform the calculations. In this software representation, the iterations in the software allow for mathematical adjustments to these layers as they calculate the best correlation based on the input data. The node on the right represents the output of a probability value.

To acquire the data, a global survey of project managers was conducted, and eighty-seven critical project characteristics were identified. The characteristics (or features) became the input to the supervised learning prediction algorithm. Next, data was collected from 50 projects that were labeled as "success" or "failure." Using the project management plan documents, the characteristics from each project were identified and converted to binary format. In other words, if a project contained the characteristic based on project documentation, the entry for that data field was a 1. If the project did not contain the characteristic, the entry was a 0. The machine learning model was a three-layer neural network and performed logistic regression based on the binary input data. An example of a user interface for a sample prediction software is shown in Figure 7.3.

**MENU**        **DATA**

| | | Scope clarity | Resource allocation | Milestones | WBS | Risks |
|---|---|---|---|---|---|---|
| | Project A | 1 | 0 | 1 | 1 | 1 |
| | Project B | 0 | 1 | 0 | 1 | 1 |
| | Project C | 1 | 1 | 1 | 1 | 0 |
| | Project A | 1 | 1 | 1 | 1 | 0 |
| | Project B | 1 | 1 | 1 | 1 | 1 |
| | Project C | 1 | 0 | 1 | 1 | 0 |
| | Project A | 0 | 1 | 1 | 1 | 1 |
| | Project B | 1 | 1 | 1 | 0 | 1 |

MENU buttons: Upload Data, Train, Test, Predict

**FIGURE 7.3** A Sample User Interface for Prediction Software Using Supervised Learning.

The first step in developing the software was to train the algorithm to create a model based on the labels of project success or failure. The historical datasets were uploaded, and the training process began. The algorithm performed validation to ensure the data fields contained structured data. Once the model was created, a set of test data with known results was used to verify that the model accurately represented the labels. The reference model now represented an image of project success. After this verification stage, the data from a new project was used as input, and the output was a probability of success in a percentage format for that project.

The input data was stored in a spreadsheet, but it could have also been stored in a database. The software program was written in Python. The software was hosted in the cloud and used Heroku as an interface for a Web browser. Creating the code for a neural network was fairly straightforward with modern programming utilities. (The Internet contains many Web sites that provide basic neural network code samples.) For this program, the neural network code was about ten lines. The entire program consisted of 30 lines of code. It is interesting to realize that such a simple deep learning algorithm can produce many results from such a short algorithm. (*Deep learning* typically uses a multi-layered neural network.)

## BUILDING AI PREDICTION SOFTWARE FOR PROJECT MANAGEMENT

For software, a *process flow* usually shows data inputs, how the data is processed, and the output. (This is somewhat analogous to looking inside a building and seeing how it functions.) The process flow for creating a training model using prediction software is in Figure 7.4.

# Input

- Features are identified for the projects
- Binary values (1 or 0) are entered for each historical project
- Each dataset (project) is labeled
- The number of datasets is above the minimum required

⇩

# Processing

- Datasets are divided into training and test data
- The 3-layer neural network use regression to correlate the training datasets based on the label
- A model is created
- Model accuracy is confirmed using the test datasets

⇩

# Output

- Model validation score

**FIGURE 7.4** The training process in supervised learning

### Input

For the training process, the prediction software receives access to the project management plan documents and uses NLP to identify if the specific factors are present. If the correct factors are found, then a "1" is added to the appropriate data field. If not, a "0" is entered. The projects are labeled as "success" or "failure," with a "1" indicating success and a "0" indicating a project is unsuccessful. The historical data is divided into training and test datasets. The algorithm uses the training datasets to learn the correlations and create a model. The test datasets are used to ensure that the model functions accurately.

## Processing

The input data is loaded and validated to ensure that there are no blank data fields and that the data is appropriately formatted. This is performed for the training data, test data, and unlabeled data that is the subject of a prediction. The basic process for machine learning software is to train, test, and predict. Once a probability value is produced, additional work can be performed to check any variability of the predictions by changing the features in the datasets or the hyperparameters of the neural network. *Hyperparameters* are selected by the software programmer and include items such as how many iterations are used in the training process and how many layers are in the neural network.

## Output

Once the model is created, a new, unlabeled dataset is entered, and a prediction is made based on the trained model. The prediction is a probability that the new dataset achieves the result defined in the label. The process is shown in Figure 7.5.

# INPUT

Unlabeled dataset that contains
identical data fields to the model
with current project data entered
in the data fields

# PROCESSING

The dataset is compared to the model
to generate a probability of achieving
the model label

# OUTPUT

A probability value

*FIGURE 7.5* The prediction process in supervised learning

The result is a percentage, and that can be subject to further interpretation. The are limits to a successful prediction. A 95 percent prediction of project success means that it is probably reasonable to proceed. Project managers need to decide the next actions when there is a prediction of 78 percent. For the project screening process, the prediction factors should at least be comparable to other projects, since they are derived from common historical data. Tracking the project's success results in more credibility and provides feedback to improve the accuracy of the software. The number of features identified in the planning documents is not fixed and can be expanded to include a large amount of data if this improves the prediction accuracy.

## The Future of Project Prediction Software

Predicting project success is very difficult. There are so many variables and so many factors that can go wrong in a project. Project managers are responsible for complex projects, and this process is a way to let an algorithm analyze the complexity. Experienced project managers may intuitively believe that an issue will jeopardize the project. It might be poor communication, improperly evaluated risks, or unanticipated client change requests. If the same issues appear consistently, it should be evident that a software program can be trained to identify similar situations and predict a similar result.

Over time, prediction software will be fully integrated with an organization's data. That includes historical projects, policies and procedures, strategic direction, and financial objectives. Prediction software will not dictate what projects to implement to make the organization more successful, but it will determine if the strategy and plan created for a project will be successful. The prediction software will be seamless, interfacing with all the required data, whether internal to the organization or external, using the internet to capture environmental data. Project planning and execution documents can be read using NLP to capture the values required for the machine learning algorithm. The software may also accept live streaming data from the project as it progresses. An essential requirement is a feedback loop that captures data and updates the model regularly.

Prediction software is already changing how projects are managed, as evidenced by numerous AI software applications available for managing projects. The biggest challenge is for project stakeholders to believe the prediction probability results and commit to appropriate action to achieve success. That includes accepting changes to the project methodology and adapting to further changes as the AI software becomes more advanced and significantly more accurate.

## UNSUPERVISED LEARNING FOR CLUSTERING PROJECT ISSUES

*Unsupervised learning* uses an algorithm with datasets that are not labeled to create groups or clusters, as shown in Figure 7.6. This is a type of classification algorithm and has numerous applications to projects. *Features* are the characteristics of the datasets. For example, risks are classified based on characteristics with the objective of finding a common cause, mitigation strategy, or risk response. The project manager evaluates risks in the planning stage and attempts to eliminate as many as possible before the project begins. The groups are not defined by a specific label. Risks are grouped by similarities.

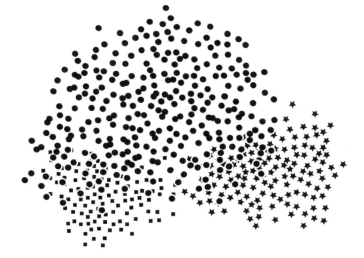

*FIGURE 7.6* Classification with unsupervised learning

Change requests are classified from previous projects to determine whether they are likely to occur on the current project. Tasks are also classified. based on the level of complexity. The complexity factors such as level of knowledge, number of subtasks, and technical skills required are identified for each project task. The unsupervised algorithm creates groups of similar tasks. Once the tasks are grouped, the project manager checks each group to see which group has the highest complexity. This process is known as *semi-supervised learning,* where the attributes of one or two tasks in the group are assumed to be the same for all tasks in that group. This is extremely helpful. If 80 percent of tasks are classified as "high complexity," the project manager reevaluates the technical skills of the assigned team members. Additional training might be required, or a mentor or coach can be added to the team. These actions are performed in the planning stage to proactively improve project performance.

A powerful algorithm to perform this function may consist of as few as two dozen lines of Python code and can reside on a laptop computer. There are many possibilities for unsupervised learning. The capability is used to detect patterns and anomalies. A risk might be missing, or an identified risk can be eliminated. Unsupervised learning also identifies stakeholder relationships that may be important for project communication. The allocation of resources can be compared to other projects and optimized. As project data becomes available when the project is being implemented, unsupervised learning looks for patterns that are useful for predicting future trends. Unsupervised learning has the potential to resolve many project management challenges.

## REINFORCEMENT LEARNING FOR IMPROVED DECISION-MAKING

*Reinforcement learning* occurs when the program learns from mistakes and avoids making the same mistake twice. This is useful in learning to play a game or finding a path through a maze. From an initial starting position, the algorithm plots the way through a maze to the exit, which is the objective. The program detects dead ends and searches for better alternatives. Let's consider how reinforcement learning can be used in project management with a project issues report. When a new issue is identified, the algorithm searches for any previous similar issues and determines what solution to avoid.

Anyone can start their own project issues database when involved in a project role. As shown in Table 7.3, a typical set of fields includes a description of the project issue, project situation, project environment, any external factors, decision taken to resolve the issue, and if the resolution is successful. If a similar problem occurs later, the spreadsheet indicates a potential solution or one to avoid. In project management, this is known as *project experience*.

**TABLE 7.3** Capturing data for reinforcement learning

| Project | Issue | Project characteristics | Project environment | External conditions | Decision | Decision success (Y/N) |
|---------|-------|-------------------------|---------------------|---------------------|----------|------------------------|
|         |       |                         |                     |                     |          |                        |

Capturing project decisions is a simple way to create data that an AI algorithm can use to improve project performance. Consider how valuable this data would be if every project manager collected results on every project for the previous ten years. Algorithms could access the data to help project managers make better decisions. (Imagine if a project manager never made the same mistake twice!)

Reinforcement learning is not at the top of the list for machine learning in project management because supervised and unsupervised learning are easier to work with and provide statistical results. Reinforcement learning may require significant amounts of data, and the results describe what decisions to avoid better than what action will be successful. With sufficient data, a reinforcement learning algorithm is powerful software for helping project managers make good decisions.

## EXAMPLES OF MACHINE LEARNING SOLUTIONS

Using machine learning for prediction and classification can improve many areas of project management. Some examples help explain how the solutions can be configured.

### Building AI Stakeholder Management Software

A typical data flow for stakeholder management software is shown in Figure 7.7.

# INPUT

- Stakeholder register
- Stakeholder thresholds
- Stakeholder personality assessment
- Stakeholder emails, messages, verbal capture, social media activity

# PROCESSING

- Develop optimum communication method
- Evaluate stakeholder risk to project performance

# OUTPUT

- Customized stakeholder communication plan
- Probability of stakeholders issues

**FIGURE 7.7** Stakeholder management prediction process

## Inputs

The inputs start with the stakeholder register and categorizations, such as the position in the organization, level of influence over the project, and desired role. Next is to document the analysis of the stakeholder threshold limits, which includes items such as the budget, schedule, risk, and quality. If possible, it includes probable reactions to exceeding the stakeholder's threshold level in any of these areas. For example, a project sponsor might become agitated if the project exceeds the threshold level for funding. As the project progresses, the overspending on tasks can be much greater than a threshold level, and the stakeholder may request action or a more detailed review of the project about future expectations.

The input may also contain a stakeholder personality assessment. Stakeholders can submit to a personality assessment such as Myers-Briggs, or a software program can assess the personalities based on a series of text documents such as emails. Third-party personality assessment software that creates a profile based on personal emails, texts, social media profiles, or any documents created is readily available (Crystal Software 2024; Faception 2024; Humantic AI 2024). There also needs to be a project management vocabulary that can be used to understand the language of project stakeholders. Project language has some unique words and phrases that are not easily understood outside of a project context. Streaming input includes the stakeholders' emails, text messages, audio capture, or social media posts collected using the organization's systems or externally by accessing the information regarding sites accessed by the stakeholders and posts on Internet sites. (This assumes that the organization allows AI software to access the data.) Table 7.4 shows an example of a typical stakeholder register, although it may differ depending on the project and the organization.

**TABLE 7.4** Sample stakeholder register headings

| Stakeholder | Role | Title | Expectations | Impact/ Power | Threshold or Tolerance Limits |
|---|---|---|---|---|---|
| | | | | | |

Table 7.5 adds headings that capture information that makes a machine learning algorithm more valuable.

**TABLE 7.5** Sample stakeholder register with additional headings for AI

| Stakeholder | Personality Type | Current Sentiment | Communication Style |
|---|---|---|---|
| | | | |

## Processing

The algorithm determines whether a stakeholder's communication is positive or negative toward the project and the project manager. The processing uses the inputs to determine an optimum communication method based on stakeholder characteristics. There is also an evaluation if the stakeholder will have a detrimental impact on project performance.

## Output

The output is a probability that the stakeholder will create issues detrimental to project success. The analysis also delivers a recommended customized communication plan to manage the stakeholders. This is the ability to influence the stakeholder in the most effective way.

## RESOLVING PROJECT ISSUES SUCCESSFULLY

Projects are very complex, and regardless of careful planning, problems always arise as the project is being delivered. Machine learning software can predict issues during the project's planning phase and allow them to be included in the risk register with a proper mitigation plan. A proactive approach can resolve the issue before it affects the project. Despite a prediction, issues always need to be resolved, from potentially minor problems, such as an absent team member, to more significant problems, such as the client having a different and conflicting interpretation of the scope statement. Having machine learning software that supports good decisions when issues arise is an ideal use for AI technology.

Project managers typically hold regular status meetings internally with the project team, externally with clients, or both. During the meeting or even outside the meeting, issues or problems arise and are captured in a report known as the *issues log*. Nothing ever goes perfectly on a project. Developing machine learning software to manage issues and problems involves two components. The first is to train a machine learning algorithm based on previous projects to predict the issues for a newly proposed project. The program determines the likelihood of encountering a specific schedule delay. By knowing this beforehand, the issue can be added to the risk register, and a mitigation plan can be created. The ultimate goal is to be aware of all possible problems before the project begins. Project managers do not like surprises, especially negative ones, that occur during project implementation.

The second opportunity for machine learning software is to recommend the best solution for any issue that occurs during the project. Despite all the planning, unpredictable problems will inevitably happen. Machine learning software based on reinforcement learning uses historical data to find the best solution, given the nature of the project and how similar issues were resolved.

The input documents are critical and include results and the issues log from previous projects with the outcome of the action taken to resolve the issue labeled as successful or not. The project documents are also important as they define the project strategy and are used as input to train the model before the project begins.

## HISTORICAL DATA

Successful use of AI software involves utilizing sufficient historical data that is accessible and properly categorized. For example, in the issues log, the actions taken to resolve issues need to be saved and labeled as either "successful" or "unsuccessful." Historical data can take many forms, and many documents are created that can be used to improve future project processes. The objective is to prevent the same or similar detrimental issues from happening again, but studies show this does not always occur (Paver and Duffield 2019). Most resolutions identified in a lessons learned document result in either procedure updates or ways to improve communication. This outcome can make the training for machine learning software more complicated. The objective is to train the algorithm to recognize and predict similar problems in future projects. That might be done by evaluating if the actions taken after a lessons learned review have been implemented in the organization's policies. In addition, many projects do not document formal lessons learned when the project has gone well. Therefore, there is often no training data or very little training data for successful projects. The opportunity to use machine learning to manage issues is outlined in Table 7.6.

*TABLE 7.6* Using an issues status report with AI software

| Stage | Opportunity |
| --- | --- |
| Before the project | Classify historical issues with a probability of occurring in the proposed project |
| During the project | Predict the most successful solutions |
| After the project | Use issue resolution results to train the machine learning software in a reinforcement learning process |

## BUILDING AI ISSUES MANAGEMENT SOFTWARE

A typical data flow for an example of "issues-management" software is in Figure 7.8.

# INPUT

- Issues reports from previous projects
- Project management plan
- Project status
- Project environment

# PROCESSING

- Analysis of issues compared to project conditions and project environment

# OUTPUT

- List of issues and probability of occurring
- List of issue resolutions with probability of success

*FIGURE 7.8* Project issues management process

### Inputs

The process uses several documents as input to the algorithm, as indicated in Figure 7.8. Project status and action documents are critical in this process as they can be expected to contain many areas where the project failed to plan for the issues either as a risk or in the plans themselves. Similarly, the historical issues reports will contain unexpected problems that previous projects have encountered. The project environment data provides additional input and can be used by machine learning software to correlate similar circumstances and outcomes.

## Processing

Processing includes an analysis of the data, and training occurs so that the machine learning software can predict or classify new issues. The first part of training is to identify the possible problems from historical projects that have not been captured in the plans for the new project. The next training goal is identifying actions that provide the best solution for any issues during project execution. Finally, it will be important to use the results of the issue resolutions as further input to the machine learning software to ensure that the data is up to date.

## Output

The two basic outputs are identifying issues not included in a project plan and the recommended solutions for new problems that arise during the project execution stage. Machine learning software can classify similar issues and use reinforcement learning to avoid previous actions that did not provide a good outcome.

## The Future of Managing Project Issues

In an ideal project setting, machine learning software predicts problems in advance and allows the project manager to take proactive measures to prevent or resolve them quickly. Suppose an issue arises at the last moment. In that case, the machine learning software can recommend an optimum solution based on what has worked in the past and considering the current project status, the organization, and the external environment. Both of these outcomes increase the probability of project success. Eventually, this type of software will be indispensable and can be connected to the project database for constant updates to the data and further improve the accuracy of predictions.

## AI CHANGE CONTROL PREDICTIONS

One of the great values of artificial intelligence technology is the ability to access vast amounts of data, perform analysis, evaluate alternatives, and make decisions. For project management, this is a significant opportunity. Consider the implications for a change request where a new requirement is proposed, and the project manager and project team consider the impact of the change on both the budget and schedule. They collect data and respond with the potential cost increase and schedule delays. In reality, the change might affect numerous additional areas of the project, which can create unexpected negative consequences. In a situation of several change requests simultaneously, the complexity of interdependencies may be too difficult to analyze for an accurate evaluation. AI software can manage both complexity and vast amounts of data and produce a more accurate assessment of the impact of the changes on the project.

### HISTORICAL DATA

Properly formatted data should be more accessible with change control data because many organizations have good standards and common templates for integrated change control. There are two parts to consider. The first is a change request log that captures all requested changes and whether or not they are approved. The second is the actual change document, which typically provides detailed data that machine learning software can use. Data from previous projects is also important because it may contain potential changes that previous projects did not anticipate. This can result in machine learning software identifying and predicting scope changes to the current project.

### MANAGING CHANGE

AI software is ideal for managing change in a project. The two characteristics of machine learning are prediction and classification. Based on the project scope for a similar project and comparing it thoroughly to the scope of a new project, AI software can predict scope changes that will be requested. Next, based on a change request to the existing scope, machine learning software can classify the change in terms of being successfully implemented and predict the impact on the project in terms of schedule and budget as well as the other knowledge areas. AI needs to be a holistic or integrated solution, and this is an excellent example of how all aspects of the project need to be considered.

*TABLE 7.7* Using AI software for project change control

| Stage | Purpose | AI Predictor software usage |
| --- | --- | --- |
| Project Planning | Predict potential change requests | Include the success probability result as one screening criteria |
| Changes requested during project execution | Classify/predict | Include success probability as a factor for consideration |

Change requests are not limited in scope and can be process changes required to the project methodology as part of corrective or preventive action, as shown in Table 7.7. Changes can be made to project documents or policies and procedures used to manage the project. A significant concern is when proposed changes have an impact on project baselines, such as scope, budget, or schedule. Changes can also have an impact on resources, risk, or quality. AI software is used to identify alternative ways to implement these changes and try to minimize or eliminate any negative repercussions. A cost-benefit analysis of a proposed change can be done by other software, but machine learning software can predict if the analysis is within certain limits. It is also important that the analysis includes all interdependent relationships since the change may create an unintended negative side effect within or with another project in the organization. AI software needs to have a high-level perspective of the project since that responsibility is also expected of a project manager.

## BUILDING AI SOFTWARE FOR CHANGE CONTROL

Figure 7.9 shows a typical data flow for a change control prediction process. This is similar to the issues data flow, and it is possible that the same machine learning algorithm can be used for both situations. The difference is the input data provided for each objective.

## INPUT

- Change request reports from previous projects
- Project management plan
- Project status
- Project environment

## PROCESSING

- Analysis of changes compared to project conditions and project environment

## OUTPUT

- List of potential changes and probability of occurring
- List of recommended solutions for change requests

**FIGURE 7.9** Change control process

## Inputs

The inputs are similar to the issues software, but this one includes historical data for both the change request log with the results of the change being approved and the change request itself with all the data fields. Once the algorithm is trained, the data for a newly proposed project is analyzed. All relevant sections of the project documents are used as input since this aligns with the holistic approach required by project managers. Perhaps the change request will have an unexpected impact on a risk. The project status is used as a basis for understanding the implications. Historical documents will be significant because problems from previous projects might indicate that a change is required to the current project.

Change requests are usually well organized and implemented in a controlled manner in most organizations. There is an opportunity to increase the amount of valuable data captured in each change request document, including the method used to implement the change and an evaluation of the success of the implementation. The machine learning algorithm needs access to all the appropriate data to produce accurate results. Therefore, the change request form may need to be updated to include additional content.

## Process

Processing includes training an algorithm to recognize a scope statement that subsequently had to be adjusted to achieve the project objective. The machine learning software can predict potential changes that impose a risk on the project. The machine learning software uses classification to help identify the most successful method to implement the changes. This might include factors such as the least cost, the fastest implementation, or different criteria if desired by the organization.

## Output

Ideally, machine learning software predicts probable changes before they are requested. This prediction is based on similar previous projects and the project status. The software should also predict the probability of success of the change based on having a positive or negative impact on the project baseline. In addition, where an implementation path is uncertain, the machine learning software can recommend the optimal solution for making the change while minimizing the impact.

## The Future of Change Control Software

A predictive analytics algorithm can be used to identify the impact of a change on all aspects of the project. Change requests typically highlight the implications for cost and schedule and then underestimate or ignore the impact on risk, quality, resources, and other aspects of the project. Fully functioning AI software for change control can predict changes at the start of the project, allowing them to be added to the risk register. Changes are evaluated and assessed during the project with the probability of the change being successfully implemented. Change in some project environments is constant, so changes in the project plans should always be expected. If a project is subject to a continuous and significant number of unexpected changes, then the project methodology probably needs to be adjusted to accommodate this situation. AI software can predict or classify expected changes, resulting in a more realistic scope statement that can be delivered on time and within the budget.

The application of AI capability will only be limited by our imagination. Managing a project is a complex activity. There are undoubtedly aspects to performing these activities where AI software can make a significant contribution, and yet it is important to consider all the possibilities. Is there a trade-off between software that makes tasks more efficient and software that takes a higher-level perspective? Project practitioners need to think differently and not assume that AI will only be able to make each process or each task more efficient. A proliferation of AI-based software for project management is underway, and decisions are required regarding the best approach for an organization to acquire software to utilize for their processes.

## QUESTIONS

### Review questions

1. How does a project manager take advantage of project success or failure predictions?

2. Explain the possible uses for classification on a project.

3. What criteria are important for using reinforcement learning?

### Discussion questions

1. Will supervised or unsupervised learning provide better predictions in projects?

2. How can project decisions be improved by using AI?

3. What additional areas of project management can take advantage of supervised or unsupervised learning?

4. How does reinforcement learning help with decision-making?

## REFERENCES

Crystal Software (2024). *https://www.crystalknows.com/*

Faception (2024). *https://www.faception.com/*

Holst, A. (2019). Artificial Intelligence (AI) Funding Worldwide Cumulative Through March 2019, By Category, *Statista, 8*(19), *https://www.statista.com/statistics/943136/ai-funding-worldwide-by-category/*

Humantic AI (2024). *https://humantic.ai/*

Paver, M. and Duffield, S. (2019). Project management lessons learned "the elephant in the room." *The Journal of Modern Project Management, 6*(3).

Thomas, N. (2019). An AI pioneer explains the evolution of neural networks. *Wired* 5(19). *https://www.wired.com/story/ai-pioneer-explains-evolution-neural-networks/*

# CHAPTER 8

# IMPROVING PROJECT PRODUCTIVITY WITH NLP

*N*atural language processing (NLP) is the ability of software to analyze and interpret communication. NLP is an AI capability that improves when combined with machine learning algorithms to create large language models (LLMs) that can interact with people. NLP capability includes document analysis, sentiment analysis, translation, and the use of a virtual assistant. The virtual assistant provides an interface to find project information. An in-depth analysis of project information can be further refined by software with generative AI.

Software applications based on NLP are available to improve project productivity. Using NLP, the software can schedule a meeting based on participant availability, sort and prioritize emails, create a project status report, and capture and distribute meeting notes based on conversations. These functions increase productivity but are also used in any general management function. Further investigation is required to evaluate how NLP capability applies specifically to project management.

## FUNDAMENTALS OF NLP

NLP began with a method known as a "bag of words" to analyze sentiment. In the bag of words method, text is *tokenized* (separated) into individual words and punctuation. Common words are counted. Let's consider an example of sentiment analysis: if the word "happy" has ten instances and the word "frustrated" is found once, this text is classified as "positive." If, after a project team meeting, the NLP software detects high word counts for the words "frustrated," "confused," and "uncertain," the project manager needs to review the communication. The message to the project team was unclear, and action is required to improve communication.

Natural language processing is a technique that treats words as data and performs analysis of the data to understand it. Python has a Natural Language Tool Kit (NLTK) that contains helpful processing functions, and it can apply statistics to the words so they can be analyzed and used in prediction and classification. Another Python library app is spaCy which can process larger volumes of text at higher speeds. The purpose is to build effective models and production-level software that takes advantage of NLP concepts. Although the apps have advanced capability they start with the same basic function. The process includes several steps, such as removing words that do not add value, such as "the," "a," "and," and similar words. NLP identifies words as the correct parts of speech, including nouns, verbs, adjectives, pronouns, and adverbs, which is important in interpreting phrases and sentences. NLP capability also includes the ability to identify *named entities*, which include proper names, organizations, locations, time expressions, and quantities. Identifying named entities helps interpret text but can also be used to match the entity used in a verbal expression to an entity in a document or detect the project name in an email.

A common machine learning algorithm in text classification is called *Naive Bayes*. It is based on Bayes theorem, which is used in statistics to predict the probability of an event based on a specific condition. In Naive Bayes classifiers, the events are considered independent or naive, meaning the classification is performed independently of previous results. NLP categorizes text or text documents as belonging to one group or another based on themes or content. While the equation can be challenging to understand, the coding is easy in Python and can be performed by importing the module desired.

Parts of speech tagging is essential for language translation and the interpretation of content. The location of adjectives and adverbs can change the meaning of a sentence. Recurrent neural networks (RNNs) can perform forward and backward analyses of sentences and phrases. RNNs also have the capability to retain a word or phrase temporarily in memory as part of the process to help interpret or translate the content.

NLP technology allows a computer to interact with a human using language. When a person speaks or creates written text, such as an instant message or an email, it is called an *utterance*. People, however, are inconsistent and can make the same request in different ways. NLP software classifies utterances to determine an *intent*. In Figure 8.1, the utterances are classified to provide weather information.

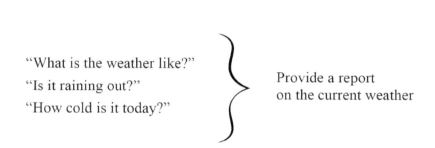

# Utterance                          Intent

"What is the weather like?"

"Is it raining out?"                  Provide a report
on the current weather
"How cold is it today?"

**FIGURE 8.1** Classifying utterances into an intent

The software also searches for variables called *slots*. These are part of an intent and identify a characteristic that has alternatives, such as today, yesterday, or next week, or identifying a person's name that is contained in the utterance. A default response is included in the software so that there is always a response. A typical default response is, "Sorry, I seem to be busy right now. Try again later." Figure 8.2 describes the response process.

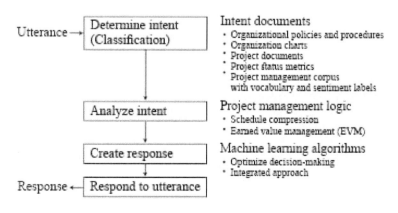

**FIGURE 8.2** The NLP response process

Based on the utterance, intent, and slots, NLP software searches for an answer based on similar intents and delivers the response. This process is the basis for virtual assistants. The purpose of using classification is to identify queries that have the same intent or meaning, and some project management examples are listed here:

- What is my next task?

- Give me my next tasks.

- What task should I work on next?

- What activity should I work on next?

These queries all relate to the same idea, and the AI software identifies and responds to all of them with the same response: the next project task assigned to this resource.

The response framework, the core part of the software, was developed to match the intent to the appropriate content in a database. This is where logic is required to select and compose the response. The virtual assistant needs to be trained to recognize the various utterances that mean the same intent, and as always, there must be a feedback loop that provides constant improvement and updates.

## DOCUMENT ANALYSIS

*Document analysis* is one of NLP's most underrated capabilities. The software evaluates a scope document to detect errors and omissions. For example, the scope could require creating a function but never testing it. Alternatively, the document might plan for a functional test without a reference to creating the function. The project management plan might be missing a risk register, a resource allocation strategy, or a failure to plan for training before the project outcome is handed over to an operations function. NLP is used within documents to improve consistency and can also generate documents such as scope, risk, and quality plans based on documents from similar projects. Layers of logic are required, but the capability requires interpreting the words, phrases, and sentences related to the document's purpose.

Finding errors and correcting them is only the beginning of NLP document productivity. Using NLP, the inconsistencies are discovered up to 20 times faster than a human project manager *(https://scopeMaster.com)*. Project managers already know proper planning is essential for project success, but there is often not enough time at the start of project to accomplish this. NLP can address the time challenge at the beginning of the project. For a software project, standard project characteristics or function points can be used to calculate an estimated cost and duration. This is important because studies reveal that 35 percent of defects in production are due to errors in requirements (Krasner 2021).

## SENTIMENT ANALYSIS

*Sentiment analysis* uses NLP software to interpret language and, when attached to machine learning algorithms, performs prediction or classification. For example, recommender systems suggest what books or movies a person might like based on descriptions of previous selections. For project management, sentiment analysis has many capabilities.

1.  An analysis of documents, such as a scope statement, can be evaluated to determine whether it will likely result in a positive or negative project outcome. This is accomplished by using classification similar to classifying images. The method is to assess scope statements used by successful projects and compare them to scope statements that have caused significant project problems. While it may seem obvious to an experienced project manager who identifies gaps in a document, a machine learning algorithm has superior capability. How much detail from previous projects and documents can a project manager remember? A machine learning algorithm can input and analyze hundreds or even thousands of previous projects and identify key elements likely to create project problems.

2.  An analysis of organizational emails and instant messages can be performed to evaluate if the project team's sentiment about the project is favorable or unfavorable. This can be used as a feedback mechanism to evaluate the effectiveness of project communication.

3.  An analysis of organizational emails and instant messages can be performed to validate or initiate actions to manage project stakeholders. Sentiment analysis detects changes in stakeholder

engagement and recommends corrective actions. The analysis can provide valuable information for a project manager who receives early feedback that a stakeholder who was positive is now resistant to project implementation. This is undoubtedly an area of controversy based on privacy concerns. The scenario describes what is possible, not what may or may not be ethical. An organization may decide that any content that uses internal computer systems should be accessible by AI software programs.

To classify the data into a positive or negative sentiment, a repository that has labeled data is accessed. In other words, there is a file of content that contains positive comments and another that contains negative comments. The content in these files is used to compare a new incoming text. Before performing this function, it is best to nullify the impact of project management jargon. A list is created that contains neutral words or phrases. The software is trained using a machine learning utility, and then test data is supplied to validate the model. The accuracy of the results depends on numerous items, and the amount of quality training data is the most significant factor. Once an accurate model is built, it can be helpful for project managers.

Monitoring project communications in an organization uses all communication mechanisms as input. This includes emails, instant messages, and other documents that may be produced. It may also include smartphone conversations, text messages, or any verbal communication captured. All communication can be converted to text, making it more easily searchable. The first step is to filter all text input to capture the content that relates to the project. The analysis can be accomplished by searching for keywords such as the project name or proper names of project team members and the project sponsor.

## STAKEHOLDER MANAGEMENT USING SENTIMENT ANALYSIS

Managing stakeholders is one of the more challenging tasks for a project manager. AI software can assist with this responsibility. The process of managing stakeholders is complex, requiring the ability to understand project management vocabulary as well as the ability to identify different stakeholder personalities. An AI-based assistant can create output that can optimize personal interactions on the project. Using NLP-based analysis on people can be invasive, but it can also be rewarding and motivating. Several creative AI software solutions are being developed commercially, but they should include privacy and ethical considerations to succeed. Overall, sentiment analysis offers an opportunity to vastly improve team members and all stakeholder communications.

Project management has its own unique terminology. Words such as "scope," "schedule," and "risk" are frequently used by project managers. Phrases such as "earned value," "schedule delay," and "scope creep" are also commonly used on projects. Project managers can utilize sentiment analysis to assist with validating the effectiveness of a new communication strategy by evaluating the words used by the project team. The project manager can also monitor project communication to respond proactively during the project and better address any challenges.

Sentiment analysis software may seem invasive, but it is currently being used for other purposes. In marketing, consumers are tracked to capture their preferences. Location analytics and facial recognition are being used by retailers and mall owners to track and measure customer shopping behavior (Rieger 2018). The resulting evaluations help to optimize store performance and ultimately increase profits. Within an organization, employees might be required to provide consent to allow the tracking of their words and activities. Sentiment tracking software will likely be used in an organization for general purposes before being used for project management. It offers a project manager an enormous advantage over existing methods to communicate with stakeholders and proactively address issues.

Every project has numerous stakeholders, from team members to customers and others in the organization who are invested in the project outcome. Unfortunately, there are some stakeholders want the project to fail or denigrate the project manager. Project managers must find a way to be successful within their organization, regardless of office politics. Some stakeholders have legitimate concerns as the project makes progress, and they often have threshold limits, for example, to the amount of risk, potential cost overruns, or delays in the completion date. In all these situations, using AI to manage stakeholders is valuable for resolving problems and reducing the stress level of the project manager and the project team. Of course, there are supportive stakeholders who promote the project objectives with enthusiasm. AI software can make suggestions to the project manager on the best way to communicate with all stakeholders, regardless of their attitude toward the project.

The purpose of AI software for stakeholder analysis is to help the project manager proactively manage stakeholder concerns. It also allows the project manager to communicate more effectively with stakeholders since AI software can inform the project manager about the best communication style for each stakeholder based on their personality profile. There are three major components to this type of algorithm. The first is an assessment of the stakeholders, including their personality type and any threshold or tolerance limits. These can be determined easily outside the algorithm but can also be assessed with AI software that is more commonly used for marketing to individuals. The second component is sentiment analysis, which uses various sources directly produced by the stakeholder, such as emails or instant messages. It assesses positive, negative, or neutral feelings toward the project or for a specific aspect of the project. Finally, given a proper evaluation of sentiment, the project manager will receive guidance on communicating effectively. With a Myers-Briggs personality profile, for example, the best way to communicate with an extrovert is not always the best way to communicate with an introvert. If a stakeholder is highly negative, the project manager can take action to diffuse an issue before it becomes more serious.

There are unique situations where stakeholder management software is beneficial. An employee working on the project may appear to be under severe stress. If the stress is not due to project issues, it can still affect work performance. In this situation, potential changes to responsibilities can exacerbate a mental health issue. Stakeholder analysis software can find the best way to communicate without adding further stress. A project team member returns to the workplace after a week away due to a personal family tragedy. A project manager needs to know the exact words to say such in difficult situations and an AI-based assistant can provide the most effective and empathetic words to communicate. An AI-based solution optimizes the interaction with project team members by helping project managers understand what to say in every stressful situation.

Another possibility is constantly scanning employee communication and categorizing sentiment to provide the project manager with clear and timely recommendations about addressing various issues. This analysis may become indispensable to the organization. The challenge is determining whether the benefits outweigh the privacy concerns. The next step is to monitor employee actions outside the workplace, which is already in place for social media posts for several organizations. This is implemented legally by creating a policy and informing employees. In many cases, an expected level of professionalism from employees at all times in the public is expected. Think of professional athletes who received discipline for behaving poorly outside their usual place of work. Similarly, a project stakeholder can be monitored while conversing after regular working hours or even while not discussing work-related activities. The acceptance of this level of scrutiny will be determined eventually by either employee acceptance or government intervention.

Searching social media for information about a project or a stakeholder is fairly simple. Searching for content related to a stakeholder only requires about four to six lines of code. The first step is to verify the social media data matches the identity of the stakeholder. The point illustrates how simple and feasible it is to scrape information from social media to perform further actions such as sentiment analysis. The organization must define what level of sentiment analysis is required or permitted. High-level tracking and summarization of results where the users remain anonymous is less invasive and still provides valuable information, such as the trend of positive or negative feelings toward the progress of the project. Tracking on an individual basis is far more effective but may lead to ethical and legal issues. Individuals may not want to work on a project that uses this type of tracking, and people who are not project stakeholders may be very negative about monitoring employees while they are not at work.

Individual tracking software is likely to be the most controversial for ethical issues. Is it acceptable to deploy an algorithm that reads and analyzes personal emails and text messages? Perhaps this would be acceptable for an organization that has an "open" culture, one that is determined to have successful project results, or an organization that places project success above any other metric. The purpose of this section is not to judge the ethics of any organization or AI-based solutions, but to present the capability that is available.

There is a possibility of having microphones in project meetings and capturing conversations. Some project meetings are recorded deliberately to retain accurate records of decisions. An alternative use would be to capture dialogue and analyze sentiment. That might seem more invasive and have implications for the level of communication that makes an individual feel uncomfortable contributing. While this topic will not be further explored in this book, it does reveal how disruptive AI can be in the workplace.

Making the sentiment results anonymous is one solution to addressing the ethical concerns. In other words, the project manager may report a sentiment trend by a grouping of stakeholders without actually knowing the names of the stakeholders. Similarly, the project sponsor can access sentiment analysis results that illustrate the trend across all stakeholders or within the project team. This can be used proactively to address issues and improve the project culture and relationships.

## THE PROS AND CONS OF SENTIMENT ANALYSIS

Here are two examples of how powerful NLP can be. The first example is about children under the age of 8 who are unable to properly express emotional suffering. Adults have the responsibility to recognize problems and seek treatment for the children in their care. Recently, an AI was developed that can detect depression based on a child's speech. With the early diagnosis of depression, children responded well to the treatment (University of Vermont 2019). The second example is from the *New York Times*. Voice analysis software was created that not only understands human speech but is also capable of detecting post-traumatic stress disorder (PTSD) (Philipps 2019). The algorithm is trained to listen for minor variables and auditory markers that are imperceptible to the human ear. The algorithm can diagnose PTSD with 89 percent accuracy.

Based on a person's voice, AI can detect mental illness and possibly other medical conditions. For example, it may be able to determine if a person who slurs their speech during a tense project status meeting is having a stroke. The potential for sentiment analysis goes significantly beyond positive or negative feelings toward a project. Voice analysis software identifies when someone is nervous about being able to achieve the end date for a task but does not want to reveal any problems. People who are overly aggressive on goals or claim they can perform more work than they can perform will be evident to AI software. While this may seem invasive to a person's privacy, if the goal is to increase project success rates, why not implement them? There are many workshops, courses, and published research on how a project manager needs to improve interactions with people, and an AI solution may be invaluable. Businesses must decide whether there is a difference between a well-trained project manager detecting a problem in a person's commitments versus a well-trained machine learning algorithm identifying the same condition.

Facial recognition is being used to identify a person's age, gender, and even emotions at a moment in time. Will this be a standard process with project stakeholders to manage them effectively? AI will test the limits of what organizations are willing to accept regarding how people are managed while working on a project. The question faced by organizations is whether improvements justify the method used. A positive benefit to the project outcome, the project manager, and project team members may outweigh any concerns about the invasive approach. People wear smartwatches to track or maintain a healthy regimen. The goal is to transfer that to a project team where a more positive environment is created, increasing the probability of project success. Employees may not want to be on a project that is consistently over budget and running behind schedule.

Technology can be used for purposes other than what it was designed for, which can easily happen in this situation. Project managers may try to find a way to replace team members who are too nervous and not forthcoming or mold a team into people who are driven to succeed. The same software that can create a positive and sharing project team environment can do the opposite based on how the data is used. Privacy will still be an issue if the organization cannot maintain confidentiality of the personal information. For example, an employee might be having a "bad day" and not be particularly friendly, although this would not be their typical behavior. The personal information gathered for analysis should not be made available to other people, organizations, or social media. It is difficult to predict what level of implementation of sentiment analysis will be acceptable and how the organization will use the results. Regardless, this is powerful AI software, and successful project teams will find a way to achieve the benefits while avoiding pitfalls.

## IMPROVING PROJECT TEAM COMMUNICATION

Machine learning analysis can make people more productive by communicating directly with them. Virtual assistants like Siri and Alexa frequently add phrases designed to appeal to humans. Phrases such as "I hope you have a good day" or "Enjoy your evening" unexpectedly added to the end of a chatbot conversation can seem endearing to the listener. An analysis of project team utterances results in an output of positive and encouraging words. AI can humanize communication in a creative and playful way. That should also be one of the goals for NLP in project management. For example, when a team member completes a task in one vendor's tracking software, a digital work of art could appear on the screen as a reward. Health monitoring products, such as smartwatches, utilize creative ways to encourage people to exercise and give encouraging messages when goals are achieved. Research suggests that some students are encouraged to perform better when courses include gamification (Chen 2015). They earn badges for completing simple tasks such as reading the course outline and the schedule for course content. Praise is given for answering questions correctly and quizzes correctly. The purpose of this section is to illustrate that machine learning and NLP can have a positive impact on people by analyzing communication and then responding appropriately.

### A Possible Scenario for Sentiment Analysis During a Project

Let's consider how AI software could supply useful sentiment analysis in a workplace.

A project team member sends the following email to a coworker: "I am not happy with my assignment. I do not have enough experience to complete these tasks on time."

Since this is a work email, sentiment analysis is performed on the document. The phrase "not happy" is a negative expression. This is categorized as a negative sentiment and included in the general project sentiment trend indicator or highlighted to the project manager, who can decide what actions to take to monitor or remediate the situation.

### Personality and Bias

It is important to analyze the project status in terms of the objectives and emotions of the project team. Based on communication, NLP can assess satisfaction, stress, and frustration as the project progresses and allow an opportunity to respond or give feedback immediately rather than wait for worsening conditions. Proactively managing project situations is an opportunity when using NLP solutions. Improved communication based on individual personality is more effective than a general response (Daly 2011). For example, introverts need time to process new information. They prefer to receive prior notification with a clear topic, so they are not surprised.

People are naturally biased based on their background, culture, and beliefs. Personal bias can be different from machine learning bias. Let's consider an example of bias in the workplace. At a certain company, a senior project manager views an employee in an administrative role as less important to the organization. Some project managers may treat the person as a valuable contributor, while others do not. Personal stress or other factors may result in bias in communication and treatment of others. Machine learning algorithms develop a bias when they learn from historical information provided by humans. Proper data wrangling techniques can eliminate or at least reduce any bias. AI-based software offers an opportunity to eliminate personal bias and embrace a more collaborative project environment.

## VIRTUAL ASSISTANTS

Voice-enabled solutions such as Alexa, Siri, or Google Assistant are helpful for finding information or creating a list of personal tasks. Chatbots (or virtual personal assistants) are frequently found in a messaging format on Web sites to interact with customers searching for information. The AI-based software can recognize and interpret sequences of words and analyze them so a response can be created. The request does not have to be exact because the AI software can classify different expressions with the same intent.

Voice recognition systems that can play music on command are being used with greater frequency in the business world. This is equivalent to being hands-free on a smartphone while talking to a database. AI software can be "fed" all the organization's documents and then allow them to be queried by a voice-enabled chatbot. This is an excellent opportunity for project managers to load a scope document and allow team members the option of making verbal queries to instantly obtain data.

The next step is to find a way to properly reflect the current project status, which requires defining an update strategy, typically as a batch-style update on a predetermined schedule or a streaming update in real time. Following this, a source that can apply project management logic to the data must be found.

The process of communicating with a virtual assistant starts with an utterance. An example of such an utterance might be "Is there training in the scope document?" The software accepts this input and determines the intent; it then searches for a relationship in the content. For this utterance, the algorithm needs to find training information. "Training" in this utterance is a noun. The AI searches the project document repository for the scope document, and within the scope document, it searches for the training section. Once the training section is found, it reads the words and replies by converting the text to a verbal response.

A company may be able to "feed" all of the project management plan documents containing project management logical connections and interpretation to a voice-enabled agent. The project manager can ask if a specific task due this week can be moved to the following week. The agent replies that this is possible because the task is not on the critical path but adds that a risk is attached to the task and will increase the risk probability from 20 to 30 percent. In this example, the agent identified that the task was not on the critical path and then identified that it was linked to a risk in the risk register. Finally, it gave the project manager an update on the risk changes. The project manager can investigate further or decide whether to move the task to the following week. This is a straightforward example of what is possible. It also illustrates the concept of ubiquitous project management. *Ubiquitous* in this context means a project manager can manage a project from anywhere at any time as long as there is access to the AI agent, usually by using a smartphone app.

## HISTORICAL DATA AND THE VIRTUAL ASSISTANT

The data required to build a virtual assistant consists of several documents. The project management planning documents are used to reply to queries and remain static documents unless changed by an approved change order, which needs to be captured and updated in the database. During project execution, additional documents may be added to track the progress of the project in more detail. In addition, updates are made to the original project documents, such as the project schedule, resource calendar, resource availability, risk register, stakeholder register, and communication plan. Once these are captured and updated promptly, the documents can also be queried regarding the current project status.

Similar to AI-based stakeholder management software, a project management corpus is required to understand the specific language used in managing projects. If practical, this may be common with the stakeholder management system that uses NLP to evaluate sentiment. The most complex and intriguing document will be the one that provides the logic behind complex queries that ask specific project management questions, such as if a task is on the critical path or the best method to manage a risk that has caused a task to be delayed. Project management techniques such as those described in PMI's Project Management Body of Knowledge (PMBOK) are one source of logic, although there are many other possibilities. Software developers need to be aware that project methods can change based on academic research or practical updates to standard project practices. Projects exist in rapidly changing environments, and a logic source needs to reflect the most recent best practices and research studies.

## Inputs

An *utterance* is a verbal or text communication, and NLP can interpret variations to mean the same request. I can say, "Give me the status report," "I want the status report," or "What is the latest status?" and receive an update on the project status. NLP performs classification to match these utterances as meaning the same thing. Figure 8.3 describes the process and references used for a virtual project assistant, commonly called a *project agent*.

The organization documents, such as policies and procedures, the organization chart, which identifies the roles and responsibilities of employees in the organization, and a list of project team members, are available to the project agent. The agent can receive a query and respond based on the project management plan, organizational documents, and project logic. Deploying a project agent means that project information is more easily available to the project manager or team members, increasing productivity by reducing search times. To interpret the utterances properly, a project management vocabulary is

## INPUT

- Organization documents including policies, procedures and an organization chart
- Project management plan
- Project status
- Project management terms and logic

## PROCESSING

- Determine intent
- Analyze intent
- Create a response

## OUTPUT

- Response to intent
- Clarification of intent
- Default response

*FIGURE 8.3* Building a virtual assistant for project management

provided in the form of a corpus for project management. This reduces misinterpretation of content since project management terms can often have a unique or specific meaning.

The next step is updating the project documents to reflect the current project status. Making a project status available can be challenging based on whether live streaming data is allowed or the status requires a physical update to project documents such as the project schedule. Live streaming data would include hourly activity as the team members are performing work. The problem with live data is volatility, which does not represent actual progress. Think of a statistical distribution where the initial sample from streaming data is far from the mean in one direction. Once all the data is collected, the result is a normal distribution, but the initial result indicates a skewed distribution, leading to a misleading conclusion. Miscommunication of the project status is something a project manager needs to avoid.

## Processing

For voice communication, the agent classifies the utterances to an intent. If the intent is not understood or does not exist, the agent will ask for clarification. Once the intent is understood, the agent searches documents and issues a response. For complex queries involving project management concepts, the agent must access the logic database, formulate the best response based on machine learning output, and understand the entire project. The logic is important and can include project metrics such as earned value or resource leveling issues. The ultimate goal is to elevate the concept of ubiquitous project management to allow access not only to project data but also logic that can respond with a recommendation that is based on a holistic perspective of the project. Having a total project or organizational perspective can be a challenge for generative AI, which may be based on a wide range of unrelated project documents or having a focus directed to a specific project within an organization. Similar to other AI software, there is a need to provide data updates to the machine learning model so that it remains current.

## Output

The output, in its simplest form, is the reply given for a query, and it is based on a static document. If the query is not understood, the virtual assistant can ask questions to seek clarification and classify the query properly. If a logic source is applied, then there will be even more evaluation as well as invoking a different machine learning algorithm to determine the best solution to a complex query involving project management concepts. A simple query regarding a task on the critical path may require analysis of other factors such as resources, risks, quality, and stakeholder thresholds. This is the only way to ensure that the response includes the total project interdependencies. As a last resort for queries that cannot be adequately answered, the agent can redirect the question to another source, such as a live person or a series of documents.

## THE PROJECT ASSISTANT

A *flash briefing* is a skill that can be set up in Alexa or other agents and is similar to a podcast or a short status update on any desired topic. It could typically be a brief report on the financial markets followed by local news. It can also be created to provide updates on various types of content, such as the current exchange rates, housing market status, or latest sports results. The same concept can be used in project management to create an audio status report based on project content and results. The routine can be set up for a project agent to provide a project overview and include any metrics produced by the project reports. It can also focus on a specific topic, such as a list of and status of the current issues on the project and the results to date on achieving a resolution.

To obtain the data, a project manager must be vigilant in creating structured documents so NLP can read and interpret them properly. There may be some missteps along the way, such as when the project manager asks the virtual agent to provide the project status in front of a room of project stakeholders, and it responds with an obscure comment.

A more complicated skill will be adding logic to the project management content to provide decision support to the project manager. The manager needs to ask certain questions. What tasks are on the critical path? What risks are no longer a concern for the project because they have moved to zero probability? The assistant needs to access a logic source that interprets the project management concepts and applies them to the content from the project documents.

It is also important to create a holistic solution, which imposes another layer of intelligence to the logic. A project manager does not want a response that says that it is acceptable to delay a task that was not on the critical path only to find out later that moving it created a significant negative impact on quality. A virtual assistant is available 24 hours a day, seven days a week, which is ideal for remote workers and a globally dispersed team. Agents can give an instant response and translate information into different languages. This is useful as long as project participants learn how to properly work with them. Until the agent is fully trained and understands project management vocabulary, it will be important to phrase specific questions correctly to receive a response that accurately interprets results such as project spending and the project schedule. It will be important to be precise, for example, by indicating a specific date or time frame for a data summary. More details on how to create a good prompt are covered in the section on generative AI.

Chatbots are either stateless or stateful. A *stateless* agent assumes the conversation is with a new person, and prior history is not considered. A *stateful* agent understands that this person had a previous conversation, and that experience can be used to provide better responses and understand the utterances better. The trend is to make functions more accessible, and an intelligent virtual assistant has that capability. The agent can provide a custom solution for an organization, or in the future, there might be skill sets that can be added to existing agents such as Alexa, Siri, or Google Assistant. Finally, users should understand that NLP is confused by sarcasm, which is difficult to assess and more complex to decipher.

To develop a project agent, there may need to be a hierarchy of permissions. An example is in Table 8.1.

*TABLE 8.1* Project document access permissions

| Role/Output | Project Plans | Current Project Status | Machine learning recommendations |
| --- | --- | --- | --- |
| **Project Manager** | Read/Update | Available | Full Access |
| **Project Team** | Read/Section Updates | Available | Limited Access |
| **General Stakeholders** | Read Only | Limited availability to key activities | No access |

## THE FUTURE OF VIRTUAL ASSISTANTS FOR PROJECT MANAGEMENT

The concept of ubiquitous project management can help the entire project team improve communications. Let's consider a hypothetical scenario of a global team of over 100 people accessing the project information. As documents are updated, such as a change request log or a risk register, everyone can access the same information. There will be an ability to receive important project updates similar to how notification settings are configured on a Web site such as LinkedIn or a sales site such as Wayfair. Settings need to provide a balance of information or be customizable so that team members are not inundated with communication. An example of good messaging is when a project change request is approved, the project manager is informed immediately. The communication can be direct voice, voice message, text message, or email.

There will also be flawless logic behind the documents that support decision-making ability as the virtual assistance is combined with an intelligent agent that can search through documents to gain knowledge, gather data from sensors, and perform data mining. The project agent can identify the best task to reschedule to free up a specific resource. After reviewing all the options based on sound project management logic, the system responds with the best answer. Not only is there a response, but it will be the best recommendation for the situation. For decision-making, software such as a prediction algorithm can be integrated into project logic so the project manager can assess the successful prediction or request additional information.

A virtual project assistant allows the concept of ubiquitous project management. For a project manager, it means accessing project data easily and instantly and making decisions based on input from a machine learning algorithm. It also allows project managers to manage multiple projects simultaneously. Simply invoke the project name for the latest updates. This is an excellent opportunity for a Project Management Office (PMO), as long as the culture is open and supportive. AI solutions should be productive and promote confidence within the project team and project stakeholders. Achieving a high project success rate will solidify the AI solution as reliable and indispensable.

For project stakeholders, it can mean accessing project information without searching documents or communicating directly with the project team. This provides less distraction for the project team. The project team can also access the documents and may provide verbal input or opinions that are also accessed by the project manager. Messages can be tagged to a specific task, project issue, or project document.

An added feature for chatbots when being accessed using a smartphone is the ability to have a facial recognition capability that identifies the person accessing the project and the sentiment expressed at that time. Software exists that detects emotion based on the 42 muscles in a human face. A software program detects if a person becomes too tired to perform a task safely. Another function is detecting illness or a person under the influence of alcohol or drugs. Virtual assistants are being enhanced with other AI software, such as prediction algorithms, expert systems, and simulation software, to turn them into very knowledgeable and interactive virtual assistants. The technology will continue to develop, taking advantage of the field of generative AI and large language models.

## QUESTIONS

### Review questions

1. What is the process for NLP to interpret and respond to a request?

2. What is the value of document analysis by NLP?

3. How does sentiment analysis create changes to a communication plan?

### Discussion questions

1. How does an organization determine what communication is allowed to be captured and used by NLP software?

2. What are the limits to taking action based on sentiment analysis for project team members?

3. What project types are best positioned to take advantage of a virtual project assistant?

4. How does ubiquitous project management support an Agile methodology?

## REFERENCES

Chen, E.T. (2015). "Gamification as a resourceful tool to improve work performance." In Reiners, T., Wood, L. (eds) *Gamification in Education and Business*. Springer, Cham. *https://doi.org/10.1007/978-3-319-10208-5_24*

Daly, J. (2011). Personality and interpersonal communication. In: Knapp, M. & Daly, J. (eds). *The SAGE hHandbook of iInterpersonal cCommunication*

Krasner, H. (2021). The cost of poor software quality in the US: A 2020 report. Consortium for Information & Software Quality. *https://www.it-cisq.org/cisq-files/pdf/CPSQ-2020-report.pdf*)

Philipps, D. (2019). The military wants better tests for PTSD. AI analysis could be the answer, *The New York Times Magazine, 04(19). https://www.nytimes.com/2019/04/22/magazine/veteransptsd-speech-analysis.html*

Rieger, S. (2018). "At least two malls are using facial recognition technology to track shoppers' ages and genders without telling," *CBC News,* retrieved July 26, 2018, *https://www.cbc.ca/news/canada/calgary/calgary-malls-1.4760964*

ScopeMaster. *https://www.scopemaster.com/*

University of Vermont, (2019). AI can detect depression in a child's speech. *ScienceDaily. www.sciencedaily.com/releases/2019/05/190506150126.htm* (accessed September 8, 2019), *https://www.sciencedaily.com/releases/2019/05/190506150126.htm*

# CHAPTER 9

# GENERATIVE AI AND LARGE LANGUAGE MODELS

Generative AI and large language models (LLMs) are related concepts but refer to different aspects of artificial intelligence. Generative AI is a broader category encompassing systems capable of creating various types of content. LLMs are a subset of generative AI that interprets human language and generate a response. Generative AI can generate new music, images, and text. An example of an LLM is ChatGPT from OpenAI, which is pretrained on a large and diverse number of datasets.

Generative AI is an attempt to move closer to artificial general intelligence (AGI), where the software mimics and is indistinguishable from a very knowledgeable person. Replies to queries are meant to be realistic, so the process of searching and generating a response can take different paths and emphasize different aspects of the utterance in creating an intent. Generative AI is based on advances in NLP technology, as shown in Figure 9.1.

## Natural Language Processing: Generative AI

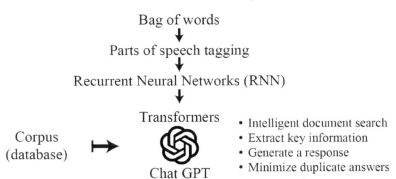

TECNOLOGY IS EVOLVING QUICKLY

Bag of words
↓
Parts of speech tagging
↓
Recurrent Neural Networks (RNN)
↓
Transformers

Corpus
(database) ➡

Chat GPT

• Intelligent document search
• Extract key information
• Generate a response
• Minimize duplicate answers

**FIGURE 9.1** The evolution of NLP into generative AI

Generative AI evolved from a simple bag of words to parts of speech tagging and RNNs. The subsequent development in software is called "transformers." *Transformers* is an AI-based technology that performs parallel processing and self-attention. It identifies key words and uses them to interpret content and create a response. The software development is most powerful when combined with the availability of a *corpus*, which is a body of work. Generative AI has access to a large amount of content because of the Internet.

Generative AI has several uses in project management. The most frequently cited value is productivity. For example, the project manager can request a scope template for a specific type of project. Document templates or samples are generated for areas such as a risk register, quality plan, or resource allocation. Templates are useful as starting points to create project documents. Additional value is obtained by generating a project schedule or budget. As the requests and responses become more detailed, productivity increases. An important caveat is that the accuracy and application of generated content need to be validated. In the initial release of generative AI, free versions generated responses that were less useful, and at times, the software would hallucinate. A *hallucination* is when the AI provides an incorrect response. An important productivity aspect of responses is to ensure that the project manager provides sufficient detail in the request. Generative AI is an opportunity to improve the quality of project planning by helping the project manager capture important content that would otherwise be missed.

A method to generate more useful content is to become knowledgeable in a new field known as *prompt engineering*. The premise is to provide clear instructions in the input so that the response is more usable. This might be considered a variation in the expression of "garbage in, and garbage out." Humans can understand a question that is asked in a variety of ways. If they are unsure, they can ask for clarification. An AI model attempts to determine the intent of a query and respond, regardless of any uncertainty. The tone and style of the response can be stated as part of the input. Some examples of the tones of the responses are below.

- professional
- friendly
- persuasive
- urgent
- casual
- funny
- trustworthy
- authoritative
- empathetic

The tones can be combined. For example, the prompt can ask for a reply in a friendly and funny way. There are numerous resources on how to use an LLM effectively. Some prompt techniques are shown in the following list.

The prompts are common for most LLMs such as those created by OpenAI, Google and Microsoft. Prompt engineering is an evolving field with a variety of prompting techniques being defined.

1. *Chain prompting.* This technique is the conversational aspect of the technology that remembers previous questions and answers. Based on this characteristic, after asking a question and receiving a response, a person can modify the next question. Using this method, the person seeks to change the first response or uses feedback to develop a better series of questions.

**Sample Project Scenario 1**

*Question 1*: What is the greatest risk to my project?

LLM answer 1: The project schedule.

*Question 2*: Why is this such a significant risk?

LLM answer 2: There are resource issues where allocated resources have insufficient experience to complete the tasks on time.

*Question 3*: What is the best way to mitigate this risk?

LLM answer 3: Assess critical path tasks by comparing task complexity to resource capability.

*Question 4*: Will there be residual issues if this risk occurs?

LLM answer 4: If the schedule is late, there is the potential for additional risks that affect product quality.

2. *Persona replication.* This feature of LLMs is controversial. By loading content from a specific individual, the LLM can assume the characteristics of the person and respond in that persona. For example, once a series of texts by a famous scientist is loaded, a person asks the LLM to answer based on the manner and knowledge of that person. For example, all the writings of Albert Einstein can be loaded into the generative AI model. That includes his books, letters, drawings, transcripts of conversations, and whatever else is available. A query is then entered with the instructions to answer as if the generative AI was Einstein. This feature of AI is a source of ethical concern. Organizations must decide if this capability will be used and what limitations or restrictions are required.

**Sample Project Scenario 2**

In Agile project methodology, customer feedback is an essential factor for iterations. With the customer's permission, the generative AI model accesses all communication, biographical data, position in the organization, personality traits, and previous decisions. The project manager asks for feedback on the project based on invoking the persona. The benefits are that it reduces real time meetings, resulting in efficiencies from both sides. The project team has the opportunity to align the project effort with customer expectations at any given time. In this scenario, the actual customer can also provide feedback at intermittent times and allow the generative AI model to be validated as accurate or updated based on the customer's responses. After receiving their permission, the project manager can load information about the customer and acquire feedback when the customer is unavailable.

3. *Chunking.* Sometimes, a lengthy response is required, and the best approach is to break it into smaller segments. For example, a person wants the LLM to write a movie screenplay. Rather than providing the basic plot and characters and then letting it create an entire movie script, it makes more sense to ask for the first few scenes. Based on the initial response, the parameters are modified before asking for the next series of scenes. *Chunking* is the process of accomplishing this request using a step-by-step approach to provide a better result.

**Sample Project Scenario 3**

Instead of asking for an entire project plan, the project manager provides the project type and objective and then requests a plan for the first stage, such as design. After reviewing the results, the next request is for details on the implementation stage. Similarly, rather than asking for an entire project management plan, the project manager asks for a sequence of components such as a risk plan, resource plan, and communication plan. Chunking allows the project manager to review the risk plan so that a prompt can be modified before asking for the resource plan.

4. *Response customization.* Additional features known as temperature and frequency penalties allow an alteration to the randomness of a response or the number of repetitive words or phrases.

**Sample Project Scenario 4**

The randomness penalty can be adjusted if the initial responses are too broad or vague. Avoiding responses that are too specific might require more creativity. The randomness can be adjusted to offer a wider variety of risk mitigation suggestions.

LLMs offer a myriad of capabilities that are being fully exploited by project managers. For example, a project manager can create a status report or an important message and ask the LLM to modify it to eliminate bias or improve clarity. Learning to collaborate with this technology using good, prompt engineering techniques improves the project results.

Generative AI software offers customization of responses by allowing participants to use their own corpus. An organization implements the generative AI algorithms with access only to its own project information. There are two main uses for this type of configuration. First, the organization can use an existing project as the corpus. Users can query the project information and retrieve accurate and timely information regarding any aspect of the project. This is valuable but also has pitfalls. Instant access improves communication with stakeholders, but some project data should not be instantaneously available. For example, a new significant risk is discovered and communicated to stakeholders before the project manager can review and determine an effective risk response. The second capability requires the organization to provide access to historical datasets for similar projects. This becomes a valuable searchable source for solving project issues. Reinforcement learning can suggest avoiding solutions that have failed in the past. Unsupervised learning can find similar problems and offer responses that are potentially the most effective solution. The historical database can be used to ensure a comprehensive list of risks is developed, or an expectation of change requests can be created.

Project managers need to validate that the response they receive is usable. Project practitioners cannot absolve responsibility by blaming AI algorithms for generating poor responses. Organizations are applying large language models to their own internal data or using it with pooled data from the same project type. Project managers need to ensure generative AI is effective at improving productivity. If the generative AI software asks for feedback, there is an opportunity to improve future responses. As mentioned previously, it is important to provide constant updates.

A smartphone app connected to generative AI increases the viability of ubiquitous project management. Managing a project from anywhere at any time includes the ability to interact with all components of the project. As generative AI continues to develop, the breadth of knowledge and accuracy of responses will increase. Overreliance on the software may initially result in a downturn in project performance. Generative AI may provide valuable information, but project managers need to retain responsibility for implementing the project.

Generative AI appears to be an easy solution for acquiring AI-based results. Load the data, ask a question, and review the answer. Using AI software that includes machine learning requires more scrutiny and a mathematical approach. A response may have received only a 65 percent prediction or classification result. The system is dependent on input, validation, and testing. If the result looks odd or needs to be adjusted, feedback should be provided to the algorithm. The system will learn what you want by constantly training it using feedback.

Understanding this process means that project managers might be more skeptical of the usefulness of generative AI results. The output from generative AI is not useless, but there needs to be a statistical approach to ensuring project decisions are made with knowledge of the potential outcomes. Human project managers make poor decisions all the time. Generative AI might increase the percentage of good decisions. Stakeholders need to be aware of imperfect responses, and project managers need to take a systematic approach to using generative AI and the results produced. Creating a draft project schedule that is subsequently modified to align with project conditions can result in productivity gains. Asking generative AI to respond to a risk that could incur hundreds of millions of dollars overrun in the project probably needs more scrutiny. Perhaps generative AI is not the proper solution, and a machine learning algorithm that produces explainable results is a better option.

The value of generative AI is most observable when the software is focused on the organization's own data. Is generic project data valuable, or should queries be screened by project similarity? The evidence is unclear. There are likely times when the project type and purpose are more relevant to the results and other times when general project information contributes more value or improves project performance. The AI system needs to learn, but the project manager and users of generative AI also need training on how to optimize the responses. Generative AI will continue to become a powerful software option for managing projects. Vast amounts of data to learn from are available and using a variety of AI-based algorithms help deliver answers that will solve project problems.

## QUESTIONS

### Review questions

1. How can a globally dispersed project take advantage of generative AI?

2. Given a project issue, what prompt methods are most helpful?

### Discussion questions

1. What process is required for customers to agree to provide their personal background information to an LLM?

2. How reliable is output from generative AI for project management issues?

3. Describe further development of generative AI that would be most useful for project management.

# CHAPTER 10

# GENETIC ALGORITHMS FOR PROJECT NAVIGATION

*G*enetic algorithms are a software representation of the theory of evolution and, specifically, the survival of species that can best adapt to a changing environment. The software code is designed to replicate the evolutionary process. Genetic algorithms are another AI-based algorithm that offer fascinating and, at times, unusual methods to solve project problems. The algorithms can be complex but provide a different perspective on managing projects.

*Genetics* is a branch of biology that studies genes, genetic variation, and heredity in organisms. Humans reproduce, and the offspring tend to look similar and have similar but not identical traits to their parents. There is no typical pattern to this process. Offspring might receive 80 percent of their genes from one parent and 20 percent from the other, or they may receive 65 percent from one and 35 percent from the other. In addition, mutations can occur. As with the evolution of any species, survival is based on those who are most able to adapt to the environment. This survival concept is known as a *fitness factor* and is essential in the project setting because it represents the project objectives. The genetic algorithm simulates evolution by creating all possible combinations of a solution until the one closest to the desired result is found. Genetic algorithms are an example of how people use nature to find new concepts and ways to solve problems.

*FIGURE 10.1* DNA strand

The genetic algorithm can be used in project management. In projects, the objectives are known, typically the scope, budget, and scheduled end date. Given the desired result, the algorithm searches for all possible combinations to achieve the objective. Figure 10.1 shows the complexity of DNA. The genetic algorithm is not constrained by human bias, knowledge, or experience. The algorithm evaluates all possible combinations of potential decisions, including solutions that a human project manager may never consider.

Genetic algorithms can be employed in project management to enhance success rates by optimizing various aspects of the project planning and delivery process. Project schedules use the *critical path* to determine the end date of a project. The critical path is based on precedence relationships, and resources are either constrained or unconstrained. Genetic algorithms can be applied to optimize the schedule based on resource constraints. Different combinations of "genes" represent the resource possibilities and are used to calculate the probability of achieving the "fitness test," which is the schedule duration (Toklu 2002). This method to address resource constraints might be more effective than other methods, depending on the project type and conditions. Resource utilization is also important when bottlenecks occur. Genetic algorithms determine the optimal distribution of resources and how to increase utilization of resources when faced with a project bottleneck (Markevich and Sidorenko 2019).

The possibilities for implementing genetic algorithms include diverse items such as feature selection and optimization, particle swarm optimization (PSO), and ant colony optimization (ACO). The challenge is to find ways to apply these to manage projects and create value by solving problems that would otherwise have a less-than-optimal solution. In projects, the desired outcome is typically to deliver the project scope on time and within the budget. The genetic algorithm evaluates different ways to successfully achieve that goal. This concept works well with constraints, which is a common occurrence in project management. For example, there is a fixed budget for resources on a project, and the project manager needs to find the optimal combination of resources to fit that budget and deliver the project successfully. Another example is having a specific duration to complete a sprint and searching for the best combination of features to include. The algorithm searches for the best solution from hundreds or even thousands of alternatives. Constraints can be any variety or combination of factors, such as customer priorities, quality, or scheduled end date. Will the proposed solution survive, and is it the best solution for this project environment? A genetic algorithm answers that question.

## FEATURE SELECTION

One of the problems with predictions based on a large number of features is knowing what features contribute most to the result. With a neural network that uses vast amounts of data, there may be thousands of features and no method to determine which of these features contribute the most toward the probability result. Fortunately, in the business world and with project management, a high volume of data is not required. The exact number of datasets and features can vary by application, but researchers and practitioners can use a low number of datasets and deliver an accurate result. The problem occurs in prediction when the outcome is inconclusive. If the prediction from a trained model is 70 percent, there needs to be a way to determine the factors that can be changed to achieve a higher prediction. Genetic algorithms offer a way to gain more insight into the factors that the prediction is based on. Some algorithms identify the subset of features that contribute the most. For example, in a study of 87 features, an algorithm returns a list of 22, contributing around 92 percent to the final outcome. Based on that result, action can be taken to improve those contributing features. However, there needs to be caution because the response should not be a simple change in numbers or text in a document to receive a better prediction. The action needs to be a meaningful change in strategy that is reflected in the updated features.

## SELECTION OPTIMIZATION

In certain circumstances, such as a vast number of possible combinations for a solution, a genetic algorithm is the best option to solve project management problems. A good example is known as the *knapsack problem*. The knapsack has a defined volume and a maximum weight to carry. These are the project constraints. The knapsack can be filled with various items, each assigned a value. The solution sets evolve in an iterative process similar to typical machine learning algorithms. With a genetic algorithm, the best solution is checked using a fitness test, which determines whether the solution meets the constraints and provides the highest value. For project management, there are already known constraints, such as a budget and project duration. An algorithm determines the optimal scope items that can be completed within these constraints. Alternately, the scope and duration are set as constraints when the requirement is to find the lowest-cost solution. In this example, resources are each assigned a cost and are added to the knapsack in the best combination.

## OPTIMIZATION SOLUTIONS

A genetic algorithm known as *particle swarm optimization* (PSO) is a method to find a solution quickly. To understand how it works, consider how a flock of 100 birds sits in a tree until they are startled. They fly up at once in a shifting pattern but never hit each other. As shown in Figure 10.2, they find a path away from the danger together. Instead of having a single project manager trying to determine a solution, the swarm represents many project managers. The swarm finds an optimal solution faster than a single project manager.

*FIGURE 10.2* The swarm effect in nature.

Another optimization problem is finding the shortest path to the end goal. In projects, the project manager tries to plot a course to achieve the objectives using a project schedule, risk plan, and other project plans. A genetic algorithm replicates this as an "ant colony." As shown in Figure 10.3, when ants are looking for food, they travel in many different directions. As ants travel, they lay down pheromones. The ant that finds a direct route to the food returns the fastest to the ant colony. Other ants notice this path has the strongest scent, and soon, all the ants discover the quickest route to the food.

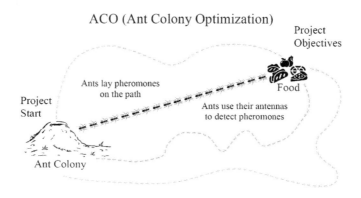

**FIGURE 10.3** How an ant colony finds the shortest path to food.

A project manager must find the fastest, most successful path to the project objective. As an organization tries a variety of project processes to deliver a project, a genetic algorithm can be used to analyze and define the best combination of activities to achieve the goal. This becomes a customization of the project method, and each organization can successfully use a method that works to complete their projects.

## THE VALUE OF GENETIC ALGORITHMS

Genetic algorithms solve different problems than machine learning software that uses neural networks to perform prediction or classification. Genetic algorithms are designed to search through a seemingly limitless number of possible solutions before determining the best one. They use machine learning in a different and clever way, mainly with unsupervised and reinforcement learning.

A genetic algorithm offers value in the following ways:

- developing creative solutions
- finding optimal solutions
- increasing the effectiveness of decisions
- requiring less historical project data

A genetic algorithm has a unique capability of "remembering" a good solution while continuing to search for other, perhaps better, solutions. If a better solution is found, the algorithm discards the previous solution and replaces it with the new one in memory. A machine learning algorithm that uses gradient descent to find correlations in the data has a weakness. In Figure 10.4, starting from the top left of the curve, the algorithm uses code iterations to move down the curve until a bottom is found. The bottom is typically determined when the next calculation indicates the curve starting to move up. In many situations, this provides a valid result. The calculation might only discover the first bottom level of a curve, and the curve continues. This is called a *local minimum*, as shown in Figure 10.4. A genetic algorithm is programmed to continue searching for a better correlation, which explains why these algorithms have great potential. The genetic algorithm stores the local minima and continues looking for a global minimum. If the global minimum is a better correlation, then that is provided as the outcome. If not, the previous minima are retained as the best correlations.

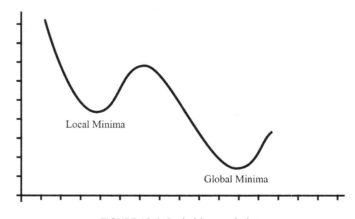

**FIGURE 10.4** Optimizing a solution

Using genetic algorithms, many possible solutions are considered, competing against each other to determine the best one, and so the data requirements vary. The algorithm starts with seed data and evolves new datasets. For a project environment, the algorithm identifies project baselines as constraints. In research settings, genetic algorithms start with a predetermined solution dataset and evolve the datasets until one is determined to be the best fit for the desired outcome. Think about a software program that can alter solution sets on its own until it finds the best one. This provides incredible value in solving problems, as the algorithm will eventually find a way to create a possible solution without human intervention. This is possible if the data is provided and the problem is framed in the correct context.

Classification and prediction are robust, but as with any technology, they have limits. Genetic algorithms offer different opportunities to make projects more successful. The evolutionary aspect of genetic algorithms also fits nicely with existing Agile projects. The Agile methodology includes a feedback loop with continuous learning and process adjustments. This is similar to reinforcement learning. The software uses a genetic algorithm to determine the most effective items to include in a sprint and identifies common risks.

## A FINAL THOUGHT ON GENETICS

The human gene pool is getting smaller, and from a biological perspective, a lack of diversity in any gene pool is a troubling trend. Research shows that genetic diversity in humans has decreased over thousands of years and is actually very low (Premo, Hublin, and Klein 2009). In project management, the equivalent analogy is not being able to think of new, different, or creative solutions. Humans become accustomed to a standard set of circumstances, and their thought processes are directed by past experiences. Ironically, although the human gene pool is shrinking, genetic algorithms are used to diversify our patterns of thinking for possible solutions to project issues. Conformity in project management drives us to lower performance, especially when faced with larger and more complex projects. Genetic algorithms are an opportunity to move beyond historical project mindsets and develop a more significant number of possible solutions much faster than humans. Collaborating with these algorithms to determine the solution with the highest probability of success vastly improves project decision-making.

## QUESTIONS

### Review questions

1. How do genetic algorithms differ from prediction?

2. What is the value of genetic algorithm capability to project management?

3. Why is optimizing a solution to a project problem important?

### Discussion questions

1. Will a genetic algorithm be more challenging to implement than a machine learning algorithm using supervised learning?

2. Do the capabilities of genetic algorithms improve the development of artificial general intelligence?

## REFERENCES

Markevich, A. V., and Sidorenko, V. G. (2019). Automating of Human Resources Management using Genetic Algorithms. *2019 IEEE East-West Design & Test Symposium (EWDTS), East-West Design & Test Symposium (EWDTS), 2019 IEEE*, 1–9. *https://doi. org/10.1109/EWDTS.2019.8884478*

Premo, L. S., Hublin, J.-J., and Klein, R. G. (2009). Culture, Population Structure, and Low Genetic Diversity in Pleistocene Hominins. *Proceedings of the National Academy of Sciences of the United States of America, 106*(1), 33–37. *https://doi.org/10.1073/ pnas.08091941052*

Toklu, Y. C. (2002). Application of genetic algorithms to construction scheduling with or without resource constraints. *Canadian Journal of Civil Engineering, 29*(3), 421–429.

PART **IV**

# *Applying AI to Project Processes*

A rtificial intelligence will deliver profound changes to project management in ways that challenge what people think is possible. To radically change a process, it is essential to understand it. Machine learning algorithms are being implemented throughout the project processes. This section is not meant to be a forecast of which AI-based software will be used to achieve an improvement in project processes. Instead, it discusses project management activities that must be completed throughout the processes and how these activities can use AI to improve project outcomes. Machine learning software must be provided with the data needed to perform the prediction and classification activities that result in better decisions and ultimately improve project success rates. This section may also interest entrepreneurs searching for creative ideas to develop solutions that improve project performance. The challenge is to think of different ways that AI can be deployed as part of each process or how AI can disrupt the overall process. These are the areas where AI is being implemented because organizations value improvements to these activities.

The review of processes is not intended to provide all the activities and nuances of a project management environment. The purpose is to prompt project managers to think about project issues in a different way and develop creative solutions based on AI capability to solve them. It is also helpful to consider the availability of data at every step of a project. Once a solution is identified, project managers need to acquire the appropriate datasets to use as input for AI software.

# CHAPTER 11

# PROJECT INITIATION, PLANNING, DELIVERY, AND CLOSE

A successful project begins with a clear requirement and is followed by a structured approach to planning, delivery, and close. These processes need to be improved by adding AI-based solutions.

## PROJECT INITIATION

The *project initiation stage* is where the concept of making a change begins, and that change requires the creation of a project. The business case or project value statement is defined and contains financial or strategic benefits that are quantifiable. The value statement should always be based on data, regardless of how much is available. The data includes business growth projections, market share, new regulations, productivity gains, and other factors that can be quantified. For a non-profit organization, it can be based on strategic values, which can also be quantified. For example, a strategic value might be implementing software to allow members to perform online self-service activities. The value statement becomes more difficult when the objective is novel, but even that has an estimated cost. The values used for all of these business cases are based on data that is available to the organization, such as cost of resources, desired growth, and increased product margins, and external factors, such as contractor pricing, resource availability, industry or government regulations, and market growth rates. Data drives machine learning results, and the data should be available for all factors, given that enough time is spent acquiring the numbers. A machine learning algorithm can also use results from similar projects, assuming there is sufficient data to validate the outcomes compared to other projects.

This stage also has a project screening or selection process where projects are either screened in for further consideration based on designated criteria or selected based on having the best values compared to other projects. The criteria might be financial, such as payback period or return on investment (ROI), which are very easy to calculate given the proper data. The probability of success can be calculated and added to the screening and selection criteria. Another opportunity for machine learning includes predicting or classifying the correct values to use for the business case and tracking the prediction of whether the values are still valid as the project is implemented. This might also be called the *project euphoria stage*. The project is approved, and is the people working on the project are happy and excited. (For many organizations, it might be the only time the project is on schedule and under budget.)

## PROJECT PLANNING

The first step in planning is to ensure a good scope statement, unless this has been completed in the project charter from the initiation stage. The work breakdown structure (WBS) is transformed into a project schedule with dependencies, durations, and resources. Various software solutions perform schedule verification, which is of great value, but unless they have a way to learn from the data, it is not authentic machine learning or AI. Budgeting and cost estimating are two ideal areas for AI, where data from the environment or similar projects can be applied to develop a more accurate budget. Similarly, contingency amounts can be acquired from a machine learning algorithm that classifies similar projects with similar events and predicts an accurate amount. Resource assignments can be complex and are usually based on the task requirements, the skill set of an employee or contractor, and, in some situations, politics. Software exists that uses analytics to match assignments to skills, although they may only offer a good match and suggest further skills training for the work to be completed properly.

Data should be available to help create a risk register and mitigating actions. Similarly, a quality management plan can be based on previously successful project outcomes, although this may be based more on simple statistics than authentic machine learning with classification. Quality in project management has two elements. The first and most obvious is whether the final product or service achieves a quality level equal to or higher than the expected quality defined in the scope document. A quality plan can include measurements taken as the project progresses to verify the internal quality, which may not be as visible, and the external measurements of the final product or service. AI software can review the quality plan of historical projects and predict issues for a new project. Alternatively, AI may have the capability to discover anomalies that have a negative impact on a project. The second aspect of quality, which may be less obvious, is whether the project itself, such as the project processes or methodology, is being managed to a quality standard expected of successful projects. This includes the effectiveness of communication, timeliness, and accuracy of status reports, as well as responding to newly reported problems that arise during the project. The project management plan should also include a way to monitor any changes to the business case. The project plans created during this planning stage need to be accurate and comprehensive. As suggested previously, the project methodology needs to access AI software to achieve higher project success rates. AI-based software improves the quality and consistency of the project processes.

Using a contracting process is an effective way to acquire resources. Procurement is a good candidate for AI software, and some solutions are making their way into this process outside of project management. For large projects, procurement typically includes either the creation of a request for proposal (RFP) or a proposal response, and both are ideal opportunities for NLP analysis. NLP identifies errors, omissions, or weaknesses in the documents. NLP also takes far less time to analyze a document than human resources assigned to the task. Machine learning software assesses the external environment or RFP responses and evaluates the optimal fit for a supplier.

One of the most critical areas in project planning is identifying risks and developing a risk management plan. However, numerous methods for assessing project risks are still based on calculating probability and impact, a popular concept in the 1980s that requires some updating. When checking the list of project risks for a completed project, the risks either happened or did not happen; this is proof that risks are binary. As the world moves rapidly to a data-driven approach that takes advantage of AI technology, there needs to be a new paradigm for managing project risks. Using data and AI software means identifying the exact conditions if the risk will occur or will not occur. In other words, the probability is either 1 or 0.

Risks are not random events, like games of chance (for example, a winning lottery number is randomly generated). Project risks are based on factors in the internal and external environment, where if there is sufficient data and data analysis, a binary decision can be made for probability. This process is available and used for infrastructure projects. Having people assign a probability to a risk is full of human bias, adding another subjective value to the project plans. AI software that is trained to analyze risks reduces or eliminates this bias.

For skeptics who think risks are random events, here is an analogy. There was a significant wind storm recently, and there was a potential for a large tree to fall on a house and create damage. The winds were 60 mph (80 km/hr.). The tree was swaying and bending severely with each gust. The risk was binary: either the tree would survive, or it would break and fall. To determine the binary result, data could be gathered on the exact type of tree, height, width, age, number of branches, and soil conditions for the roots. Then, data could be collected for similar trees, and the results obtained with identical wind conditions. The data could then be used to determine the binary risk of the tree surviving. What about a situation where the probability indicated a 20 percent chance of a tree falling over? Is that a random probability or a lack of data? There is a new way to manage project risks in a digital world. The data needs to be collected and used to create a binary risk probability of 100 percent or 0. It will be an arduous task until statistically significant results can be generated.

The first step to a binary risk plan is to collect risk data. Historical data, the current project conditions, and the future project environment are three categories of data necessary for binary risk management. The process starts by collecting historical data for the following items:

- the specific risk
- the project conditions
- the environmental conditions
- whether the risk occurred or did not occur

The next step is to identify the risks in the current project and gather data about the project and environmental conditions. Once the data is collected, a machine learning algorithm uses classification to analyze risks to determine whether they will or will not occur.

Can all risks be classified as binary? For now, the process only needs to be better than the old processes. Using regression analysis, it is always possible to incorrectly classify a risk. Based on more accurate predictions, risks either become part of the project scope, schedule, and budget baseline or are ignored. There is an argument that no one can predict the future. Yet, people make accurate predictions all the time. If people go outside when it is raining, they know they will get wet. Predictions can also be made for events that have not happened before. If someone walks in front of a fast-moving vehicle, they can predict they will get injured. The future cannot be predicted perfectly, but AI technology can make far more accurate predictions than humans. At least human bias can be reduced or eliminated and replaced with advanced statistical methods and data used in AI technology.

## PROJECT DELIVERY

The project implementation process is where all the work gets done and generates the most real time data. The work consists of resources being applied to tasks over time. Of course, additional information such as quality results and risk events may also be outcomes of this stage. Changes to the project scope may be requested and approved. Problems and issues are identified. Procurement contracts can be initiated, approved, and performed. Status reports are created and shared through an appropriate communication method. This is where the action happens, and if the planning is inadequate, incomplete, or poor, the delivery process can be challenging to accomplish.

The methods may differ depending on whether the approach is waterfall, Agile, or a combination of both. Nonetheless, this stage generates the most data and variances from the plan. It is an ideal area for machine learning algorithms to access and utilize the constantly updated data to keep the project on schedule and under budget. As a project progresses, it is unusual for everything to proceed as planned. Numerous tasks are completed, and then some unfortunate events occur. Predictive analytics is used to help a project scheduler understand

and manage resources to achieve time and budget constraints. Data can also be misleading if not used carefully. For example, one task might be budgeted at 40 hours and take 32 hours to complete. Does that mean all future tasks will only take 32 hours? Of course not. Let's say the next 40-hour task actually requires 46 hours of work. It is this volatility and low sample size that makes predictive analytics difficult. Machine learning software might be a better solution if it has access to data from numerous similar projects and activities.

This stage is where most, if not all, of the scope changes occur. Whether it is incomplete or ambiguous details in the original project scope, changes seem inevitable. AI minimizes the changes during the planning process through comparisons to similar projects, evaluating typical changes, and classifying whether they are likely to occur on this project. Even if changes are not included in an updated scope at the start of the project, they can be listed in the risk register and managed there with greater confidence.

Managing resources is often the most significant issue in projects. Project managers are high-value targets for improving communication and learning to manage people. Dealing with people requires excellent diagnostic and communication skills. How can project managers learn to be more enthusiastic yet diplomatic when responding to a person's problem? AI is capable of performing a personality assessment so that the project manager has an opportunity to tailor the communication to an individual. For example, coaching a sports team is a good learning opportunity for project managers to develop communication skills. The first step in this example is to focus on listening skills. When the children on the sports team have a concern, it is best to listen carefully. Then, summarize what the child said and repeat it back to them. Continued communication and action to solve the problem are also important. The coach then takes responsibility for managing the child's problem. How does this coaching example relate to machine learning? AI classifies conversations to help a project manager make good decisions. It can identify if the concern requires action or if it is sufficient to merely listen to the child.

Two aspects of quality can be addressed in the project delivery stage. The first and most common one describes a quality management plan, which addresses how the project ensures the product or service is delivered with the expected level of quality. This can be accomplished with measurements and processes that build the quality into the final deliverable. The second part is the quality of the project management process, or more specifically, the quality of the methodology used. If a machine learning algorithm measures the success factors of projects and then compares them to the methodology used in each project, that might provide insight into how to achieve a higher project success rate. The project methodology is changing because it does not deliver a consistent success rate of 95 percent or more for all projects in scope, schedule, and budget. In larger organizations, there will be more than a single concurrent project, and there are likely interdependencies with other projects. The projects might be using a shared resource, depending on a deliverable or document to be completed at a specific date from another project, or expecting lower costs based on shared purchases of common items. The main dependencies are easy to track, but with all the activity in the project delivery stage, many of these interdependent connections can be lost. An automated system will be able to maintain a perspective and notify the project manager when there is a risk. Adding machine learning to the process allows an evaluation of the entire portfolio of interdependencies and a prediction of where weaknesses need to be resolved.

One of the most significant concepts in project delivery is the critical path. The concept needs to be updated to ensure the critical path remains relevant. The critical path was used extensively in the 1960s to enhance the project methodology for the US space program. (Project managers still look for that red line in MS Project to identify activities that, if one task slips, delay the project end date.) Using AI, the critical path can be modernized and become more meaningful. The red line only determines the longest sequence of tasks based on precedence factors. A new AI-based critical path incorporates additional criteria.

1. Assess the resources applied to critical path activities to determine whether they are adequate to complete all the tasks as scheduled. This analysis includes comparing the task requirements to the skills being applied by the allocated resources.

2. Thoroughly evaluate all the risks on the critical path on a continuous basis. Risks are troublesome issues for a project manager. AI improves the analysis and ensures mitigation is applied to critical path activities.

3.  Investigate all possible constraints that will impact the critical path. The theory of constraints offers an interesting perspective on how any activity can be delayed based on bottleneck factors.

4.  Evaluate the accuracy of the precedence relationships on an ongoing basis. As the project progresses, activity relationships may change. The precedence concept is used when recovering a schedule by crashing or fast-tracking activities. Based on data, AI reevaluates how activities are connected and the possibility of changes.

5.  Evaluate activities not on the critical path to determine whether they will inevitably cause a schedule delay. The previous points all apply to how the critical path might change over time.

The critical path is a fundamental and valuable concept in project management. With new technology, such as AI, it is time to rethink how the critical path is applied to projects. AI can process more data and provide faster analysis than a human project manager. AI software analyses all the factors in real time and informs the project manager of issues. This is an opportunity to update the critical path concept using new technology and increase expectations that the red line provides more meaning to project managers.

One concept being implemented in the delivery stage of project management is the *digital twin*. The digital twin concept is used in construction to represent a physical object. One way to understand the digital twin is to think of a large building being constructed that has a virtual counterpart detailing the exact architectural design. Building information modeling (BIM) is a vital component that renders buildings as a three-dimensional computer model. Developing and using the model is crucial for engineers, real estate developers, contractors, manufacturers, and other construction professionals to plan, design, and construct the physical building. A digital twin is a duplicate of the BIM model and is used to implement changes in the virtual model before they are added to the physical construction. The digital twin allows different changes to be made and the results evaluated for effectiveness.

In project management, a digital twin is a virtual duplicate of the project. It allows proposed changes to be made before implementing them in the actual project. For example, the project manager simulates a risk and determines the impact on all aspects of the project. The project manager can look for ways to accelerate the project schedule, implement the changes in a virtual model, and verify that the project remains viable. This is similar to performing a simulation in the software world, and the project digital twin contains an integrated model of all project components. The digital twin concept takes advantage of machine learning algorithms to process large amounts of data. Data from sensors and IoT are analyzed to detect patterns, which are used to gain insight into project performance. The digital twin concept improves project efficiency, optimizes resources, and determines how different decisions have an impact on the project results.

## PROJECT CLOSE

The closing process is more important now that organizations use machine learning algorithms. In the closing stage, the project manager ensures that all the project data is captured and stored in an accessible format. The data needs to be labeled where appropriate so that machine learning software can either access the data or use it to update an existing algorithm. The project issues report is one example of ensuring that datasets are labeled. The actions that resolve the issue should be identified as successful, and actions that did not resolve a problem should be labeled as unsuccessful. Machine learning software uses all the data to classify or predict the best action for an issue that arises in a project with similar circumstances. The same is valid for risks. At the end of the project, the risks and risk mitigation plans need to be identified with sufficient data for machine learning algorithms to use. The lessons learned actions must be captured throughout the project so the data can be applied to future projects. Machine learning software can use the data in several ways, such as for project planning and issue resolution in the delivery process. All the results must be appropriately stored as clean data, which makes it easier for all AI software to access and use. This stage of the project is no longer a low-value administrative closure. It is now an essential data collection point that has dependencies for AI software that can provide significant improvements in future projects.

## QUESTIONS

### Review questions

1. How can AI improve the outcomes for each project process?

2. How can NLP be used in project delivery?

3. How is project close different from traditional closure?

### Discussion questions

1. What process area offers the most opportunity for AI to deliver value?

2. Who should be responsible for data capture in each process?

3. What approach should be taken to incorporate AI into the project delivery process?

## CASE STUDY: PROACTIVELY MANAGING LARGE INFRASTRUCTURE PROJECTS

A construction company bids on government contracts to build roads and railway tunnels. They have multiple projects with a portfolio budget of $390 million. AI software is acquired to monitor costs and schedules as each project progresses. Project data from similar projects is used to train a machine learning model using 50 project datasets. One of the projects is one-third complete when the AI software detects pending deterioration in schedule status and budget spending. The project manager takes immediate action to mitigate potential risks and performs a complete review of resources assigned to future tasks. Subsequently, the project was completed on time and four percent under budget.

1. What value is provided by detecting early deterioration in a project?

2. What other types of projects might benefit from this example of using AI to forecast project performance?

3. Can additional AI algorithms be used in the project, or was this sufficient?

# CHAPTER 12

# PROJECT CONTROL AND PROJECT TERMINATION

The *project control process* is the critical collection of metrics throughout the project used to identify the project status. It provides important data that is used as input for machine learning algorithms. Not only is the raw or current data valuable, but derived data, such as trends, are also used. Therefore, it is important to capture the appropriate metrics, make sure the data is consistent and clean, and ensure the data is stored in an accessible repository or a database format that is readable by AI software. The basic metrics for status and schedule are always important. There will also be other input data that a machine learning algorithm needs, such as quality metrics, risk events, progress and status of contracts, change requests, and changes in the tolerances of stakeholders. Capturing the data is essential.

Budget monitoring is an excellent example of this process. A project manager needs to understand why a project is over budget. To avoid overspending, it is essential to ensure accurate estimates at the start of the project and then proactively manage the project budget by evaluating the budget forecast as the project is underway. Machine learning software that makes accurate budget predictions offers incredible value. To build confidence in a project budget, a review of historical data can reveal anomalies or variances that may not be evident. Finding a correlation in the data is precisely what a good machine learning algorithm does. Classification is used to discover a variety of potential issues with costs. The software compares a series of successful projects with the current project to identify any concerns or areas that require contingency.

Evaluating the project status requires the definition of project metrics. *Key performance indicators* (KPIs) allow stakeholders to understand project performance. For a process that uses AI-based software, predicting problems before they arise and being proactive to minimize any impact are essential actions for improving project performance. Earned value management (EVM) is an excellent opportunity for AI software to capture data and analyze trends. The critical tracking metrics are the cost performance index (CPI) and schedule performance index (SPI); it is important to monitor the trends of these metrics and compare them to other aspects of the project. Machine learning is about correlating data and, in this case, correlating project data. One possible use of machine learning is using the CPI metric to predict project deterioration and to predict it before a human could detect it. Some organizations use CPI trends in a statistical process control chart (SPC) to discover when the cost performance is shifting to an undesirable trend and take action to remedy it. CPI trends can also be used by a machine learning algorithm to detect performance deterioration based on historical datasets. The AI solution provides warnings earlier than a project manager can detect. Not only is the deterioration in cost identified earlier, but AI also determines what level of cost overrun will occur. The results indicate how severe the issue is and how strong the response needs to be to maintain the project within budget. Calculating the estimate at completion (EAC) and variance at completion (VAC) for the project requires simple math. Machine learning software, however, can verify the accuracy of the values. The project manager needs to answer several important questions about the values. What values are used for an Estimate to Complete (ETC)? Which model is best based on the project data to date? A machine learning algorithm uses historical data to ensure that the ETC and forecast of project costs are more accurate.

The same method is used to forecast a more accurate project completion date. Schedule forecasting can be challenging due to the requirement to include a calculation of the critical path and all the possible implications of critical path changes based on task durations. Using AI for schedule prediction and classification is complex, but AI software manages complexity faster than other methods. Building a learning model based on data requires a single algorithm instead of hard coding every possible branch of decision-making possibility. Schedules can also have a critical path that shifts as the project progresses. There are a series of dependencies, such as resources or other items, that impact tasks starting or being completed. Milestones are used to identify when a series of dependent tasks is completed. The complexity of the data is ideal for machine learning software, and completing a project on time is a significant challenge for many organizations. Creativity and insight are required to determine where and how AI software can eliminate schedule issues. The objective is to discover why a project is going to be late, but the schedule is simply a reflection of the impact of other factors, such as a resource issue or a risk that took longer to resolve than was planned. The project end date is based on the critical path, so the analysis needs to assess ways to manage the critical path. This is where existing solutions use methods such as checklists, simulation, and predictive analytics. The challenge will be deciding how to overlay machine learning capability to make these solutions more effective. Project research may use statistics to find process correlations or to recommend the best generic project management methodology. A machine learning algorithm finds correlations to determine the best methodology for each project based on the project objective, conditions, and environment. Instead of using theories that recommend an overall strategy, machine learning uncovers specific correlations that make a project successful by searching for patterns in the data. These might include a hidden problem unique to an organization or a project problem that only AI software can discover and reveal.

## PROJECT TERMINATION

Despite all efforts, there are times when a project is stopped before it reaches the end goal. There are times when a project is deliberately shut down and times when it should be stopped based on the project data. For example, a project is stopped because the organization or project steering committee refuses to grant more funding. Typically, this happens when projects continue to miss deadlines and need more money to pay for resources because the scope or amount of work is underestimated. Sometimes, the business case or reason for completing the project is no longer valid. One or both sides of the cost-benefit equation have changed dramatically. Either costs have increased, the value has decreased, or both. This can be difficult to assess when a project manager is in the middle of a busy delivery stage, so machine learning software with sufficient data can be used to determine the project value on an ongoing basis.

An internal issue might be a lack of skilled resources and other reasons why tasks take longer to complete and cost more. External issues include but are not limited to higher-priced materials, contracts, and declining access to resources. There may also be international laws or regulations that change and create obstacles to completing the project the way it was originally planned. A decision will be made to either defer the project or shut it down completely. Shutting down a project is difficult because people do not want to waste the finances they have already spent. Continuing to fund a project destined to fail can be enticing, which is why good project prediction software is valuable. A probability forecast based on data provides additional evidence of the impending result.

## QUESTIONS

### Review questions

1. What type of trends can AI software detect?

2. How does AI influence decision-making regarding the value of a project?

### Discussion questions

1. What additional metrics are important for AI to analyze?

2. Is an AI result more reliable than human intuition when assessing project value?

## CASE STUDY: PREDICTING SUCCESS AND FAILURE

An organization has over one hundred projects in progress at the same time. The projects have different durations and budgets. The organization is concerned about the ability to properly manage shifting priorities and decides to implement a prediction algorithm. The objective is to determine which projects provide the most significant value. Using a machine learning algorithm with supervised learning, the organization predicts which projects will achieve cost targets, which projects will be delivered on time, and which projects have the lowest risk. The machine learning algorithm also predicts which projects provide the highest value by reevaluating the business case as changes occur in the business environment. The predictions also apply to poorly performing projects, and those receiving poor results will be canceled.

1. How can the organization decide which projects should be given higher priority?

2. Are there other criteria to consider for projects designated a higher priority?

3. How can organizations determine the value of a project being implemented?

4. Before projects are canceled, should the organization review the datasets used for input?

5. How can the reasons for making a project a high priority or deciding to cancel it be explained to project managers?

# CHAPTER 13

# *AI for Agile Process Effectiveness*

The waterfall process does not suit all projects. Agile is a different approach, and aspects of the Agile methodology can be incorporated into any project process. Agile is based on iterations that produce a result, seek feedback, and adjust the project activities as required. This constant feedback loop from a customer after a sprint provides more real time data. It allows an AI algorithm to perform instant analytics to predict an outcome that may or may not require further intervention in the project management process. The waterfall approach has significantly more data in the form of project documents, which lends itself to the concept of data mining and predictive analytics. Agile does not necessarily produce less data than a waterfall project. Instead of Agile requirements and processes written in project documents, Agile data exists as less formal content such as emails, stakeholder communication, team meeting discussions, and instant messaging. If appropriately configured, AI technology with NLP can access this data.

Characteristics of the Agile process include user stories, a Scrum Master, and stand-up meetings. AI software discovers errors and omissions, calculates cost and duration, and enhances quality for managing user stories, which comprise a narrative of the scope for the project (See products such those found at *ScopeMaster.com*). Discovering errors at an early stage avoids significant delays, reiterations, and additional costs

(CISQ 2022). Cost and duration estimates are calculated using function point analysis and details extracted by NLP. An added benefit to organizations is that finding potential bugs and performing sizing estimates can be educational and help people learn how to create more accurate scope definitions for future projects.

Two challenging areas for Agile sprints are effort estimation and risk prediction. Machine learning algorithms are used in these situations because they are naturally good predictors based on regression analysis of sprint data. Supervised learning is used to correctly estimate the effort based on the details of previous sprint estimates and the results of user stories. Forecasting risks in Agile is accomplished by comparing the current health of the project to historical experience. Some AI-based software used in the waterfall process can also be adapted for Agile environments.

There are many project areas where AI capabilities improve overall performance, productivity, and decision-making. AI-based software assists in sprint planning by analyzing historical data to understand team capacity, helping prioritize user stories, and recommending backlog items to be implemented based on user behavior, business requirements, or other relevant factors. It also assists in prioritizing tasks within sprints based on factors such as business value, technical complexity, and dependencies. AI provides predictive insights into Agile project progress, helping teams anticipate potential delays or scope changes. This allows the project manager and team members to proactively adjust plans. AI optimizes resource allocation in Agile projects by considering team member availability, skills, and task dependencies. This ensures proper alignment of team members to project tasks. AI automates code reviews, identifies potential defects, and helps maintain code quality throughout Agile development cycles. LLMs are very effective at creating, modifying, or reviewing code based on receiving detailed instructions.

In Agile projects, customer feedback is crucial. AI software analyzes customer feedback, comments, and formal reviews to provide insights that inform product improvements and prioritize features in the backlog. Agile teams can use AI-powered chatbots or virtual assistants to answer common questions, provide information, and assist team members, stakeholders, and customers in real time. AI supports Agile team members by analyzing metrics related to sprint performance, user story completion, and team productivity, enabling informed decision-making during retrospectives and sprint planning. It can also generate user stories by analyzing user needs, behavior, and market trends, helping teams identify valuable features to develop. AI software can review the scope statement created by the project team to detect errors or omissions. AI-based software can create functional test requirements based on the user stories created, and it can optimize pipelines by identifying potential bottlenecks and recommending improvements in the development and deployment processes. AI can automate some functions of the Scrum Master and support other tasks by tracking team performance, monitoring sprint progress, and identifying areas for improvement. For all of these opportunities, AI software selection and integration should align with the Agile principles of flexibility, adaptability, and customer-centricity. Additionally, AI should enhance the work of the Agile team, not disrupt its core values and practices.

## QUESTIONS

### Review questions

1. How does AI help sprint planning?

2. How does AI improve Agile communication?

### Discussion questions

1. Is predictive analytics the same as AI?

2. Will machine learning or NLP have a more significant impact on Agile processes?

## REFERENCES

CISQ (2022). CISQ Publishes the Cost of Poor Software Quality in the US: A 2022 Report. *Plus, Company Updates.*

## CASE STUDY: RESOURCE ALLOCATION ACROSS A PORTFOLIO

A large corporation has many projects implemented in parallel, and priorities are constantly shifting. Two thousand resources are assigned to the project work. Some projects encounter insufficient resources for a task, others have resources that lack the proper skills for a task, and each project provides different challenges to the organization. At unexpected times, the projects face severe resource constraints due to misallocated resources, and several projects are delayed. Project delays cause significant concern from the customer dependent on achieving scheduled completion dates.

An AI-based software solution is acquired to optimize resource allocation across all projects. The software evaluates resource skills compared to activities required and focuses on optimizing on-time project completion. AI analyzes resource capability, forecasts resource requirements for tasks, and prevents bottlenecks. A critical assessment is the ability of specialized resources to move easily across project activities. The allocations are revised regularly and adjusted based on the organization's changing priorities. The number of projects delivered late is significantly reduced.

1. What problems are resolved by implementing AI-based software?

2. How does focusing on the schedule objective make it easier to accept AI results?

3. How does AI capability compare to other methods to address this portfolio issue?

# CHAPTER 14

# APPLYING AI TO RESOLVE PROJECT FAILURE

Project managers tend to be optimistic. This positive outlook is useful when starting a complex activity like managing a project or resolving issues in the project delivery stage, where considerable project manager involvement is required. Foreseeing the internal and external influences that create problems and, ultimately, project failures, such as significant overspending and constantly delayed end dates, is difficult. There is project scheduling software that improves processes using predictive analytics to determine better resource allocation and enhance scheduling dynamics. Can a solution eliminate project failure? In project management, a good plan contains sufficient detail to avoid surprises. The project team may have problems understanding different requirements and predictive analytics. An example is probability theory. When a coin is flipped three times and turns up heads each time, what is the probability that it will be heads on the next flip? The answer is 50 percent because there are still only two sides to a coin. Humans are naturally biased by experiences, but machine learning allows the project team to make decisions based on data rather than personal bias or perceptions.

*Cognitive bias* is the human tendency to make decisions that are not based on logic. In project management, optimism bias is a significant problem when determining the accuracy of project baselines. Daniel Kahneman's seminal research challenges the belief that humans make rational economic decisions (2016). The term *planning fallacy* describes underestimating task completion time and costs, regardless of available historical estimates for those tasks. Flyvbjerg expands on Kahneman's work by describing ten behavioral biases common to project managers (Flyvbjerg 2022). Research suggests that even human memories are flawed and do not provide good recall of events (Lange et al. 2021). A machine learning algorithm calculates an outcome based on data and can avoid these types of problems.

So far, the benefits of a machine learning algorithm have been expressed in terms of improving the probability of project success. This section evaluates the reasons for project failure and whether AI can address these causes. Studies of project failure list several reasons, often finding a different set of factors. The main causes commonly listed for project failure are reviewed here.

Leadership is about being confident and making the correct decisions. The easiest way to lead is to win: any sports team that wins a championship likely supports its captain. Winning tends to override any discontent or conflict within a group. The team has the same goal, and achieving that goal is special. The same is true about projects. Let's consider the example of a project manager who delivers a high-profile, complicated two-year project on time and within the budget. There may have been numerous issues along the way, but in the end, the pride of accomplishment can outweigh the challenges. The first way AI prevents failure is by providing the project manager with a high probability of winning, not only from the start of the project but also as the project progresses. With AI software, the tasks will be achievable. This is supported by a better planning stage, project strategy, and appropriate risk planning to avoid and mitigate risks. A realistic project plan with a high probability of success can support a manager's success. Using the right software provides confidence that all the stakeholders will tolerate the challenges if they believe the project will be successful.

The next problem is also related to leadership: communication. Lack of communication, miscommunication, or poor communication are often cited as reasons for project failure. Clear and direct communication possibilities will significantly improve if the project uses a virtual assistant with an intelligent agent. This will undoubtedly be an improvement for remote workers and globally dispersed teams. As discussed in the stakeholder management section of Chapter 3, the project manager will have access to recommendations that provide communication based on individual personality, which is very effective. A pulse of the sentiment for stakeholders will also allow proactive measures to prevent negative attitudes from derailing the project. These powerful techniques are being used today and will likely improve. The objective is to adapt them to be utilized for project management.

Decision-making should be the easiest issue to fix. Machine learning software can optimize every decision in the project, even if the decision appears illogical at the time. Because the ultimate objective is to have a successful project, machine learning software can be trained to "know" how a series of decisions can result in a good project outcome. Even for projects that do not finish on time or within the budget, machine learning software can calculate the best result given the circumstances. The software can track many projects at the same time and provide a variety of metrics for each project. Analytics can be used to determine which projects are performing well and which ones are not. Some dashboards give a visual display of status without indicating which metric is the most critical. More importantly, the software can track the interdependencies among projects and provide early warning of actual and potential problems. The project should not fail because a previous project missed a deadline and can no longer provide the input required to complete the connected project. Machine learning can identify which interdependencies are more likely to fail, and perhaps streaming data can be used to predict potential failures in time to make the adjustments necessary to save the project.

The project sponsor may have preconceived ideas of the scope, and these are not clearly defined in the scope statement. AI software can review and verify that the budget and schedule are obtainable given the scope and whether unidentified expectations also need to be revealed. AI-based software can check the previous history of projects specific to the sponsor and other similar personalities that have a habit of expanding or changing the scope statement. The project manager can use this information to clarify the requirements before the project begins. The sponsor may have threshold levels for various aspects of the project, such as budget overspending, schedule delays, risk, or quality. These should be noted before the project begins, and AI is not needed to calculate them. AI can identify the expected outcomes based on the project variables and hopefully reassure the sponsor that the probability of achieving the expectations is high.

Some organizations do not want a project to succeed for whatever reason. Perhaps a senior member of an organization hopes that a specific project manager will fail and helps that occur. These are project problems that machine learning cannot solve. A clear strategy with a successful prediction and risk plan can set the project up for success. Still, if organizational interference is delivered in a way that causes project failure, an AI solution is unlikely to be able to predict or avoid this.

Several academic papers outline the causes of project failure and categorize them into three groups: people, process, and communication. All of these are easily addressed by AI software. The "people" issues include being able to resolve technical project issues and involving the client or customer earlier and throughout the project to manage change. AI software can compare historical data to ensure the technical issues are adequately included. Involving the client is always a useful suggestion. An AI predictor algorithm used throughout the project helps manage all stakeholders based on stakeholder characteristics. The process issues that promote failure include poorly defined requirements, insufficient validation of project baselines such as the budget, schedule, risk, and quality plan, and a poor implementation strategy. A prediction algorithm is ideal for indicating the probability of project success based on the strategy. Software utilizing NLP can identify poor requirements.

Another category of failure is the inability to motivate the team and the lack of effort to ensure they have the skills and technology required to complete the tasks. People want to work on a successful project, and with AI software providing better documents, planning, and decision-making, team members will be more likely to be excited to be part of the project. Ensuring team members have the proper qualifications can be performed by several types of existing software without AI, although one with AI will probably be developed. If team members do not have the proper training or skills, a solution using prediction software will detect it and forecast a reduced probability of success.

## QUESTIONS

### Review questions

1. How can a project manager use AI to improve communication?

2. How can a project leader use AI to improve project decision-making?

### Discussion questions

1. Can a project manager leverage AI software in an environment where some stakeholders want the project to fail?

2. How does AI overcome the planning fallacy and human bias?

3. How much should stakeholders contribute to making decisions when AI software has been implemented?

## REFERENCES

Flyvbjerg, B. (2022). Top ten behavioral biases in project management: An overview. *Project Management Journal* 52(6). *doi. org/10.1177/87569728211049046*

Kahneman, D., Rosenfield, A. M., Gandhi, L., and Blaser, T. (2016). Noise: How to overcome the high, hidden cost of inconsistent decision-making. Harvard Business Review, 94(10), 38–46.

Lange, R. D., Chattoraj, A., Beck, J. M., Yates, J. L., and Haefner, R. M. (2021). A confirmation bias in perceptual decision-making due to hierarchical approximate inference. *PLoS Computational Biology, 17*(11), e1009517. *https://doi.org/10.1371/journal.pcbi.1009517*

## CASE STUDY: DEPLOYING A MASS TRANSIT SYSTEM

*FIGURE 14.1* Deploying a mass transit system

A capital city embarks on a project to develop a light rail mass transit system. After several false starts due to political turmoil, a proposal is generated and approved, and a consortium of vendors is awarded the contract. The city government has no experience deploying a mass transit system and relies extensively on the vendors to make decisions and complete the project. Multiple risks include existing railway lines where the new light rail system will be built, inexperienced decision-makers, weather concerns based on a cold, snowy winter climate, and the decision for a single-day cutover of the entire system. The cutover day plans to have the light rail system running, and all commuter buses will stop providing service. An unexpected delay in the middle of the project was caused by a sinkhole that opened up on a downtown street, which may have been caused by underground drilling. Sewer pipes under the city core were built in the 1800s. Regardless, the implementation schedule incurs a significant delay as tunneling is stopped for weeks until the sinkhole is repaired. The original budget for the project was $9 billion. The project finished with a cost overrun of $1 billion and was one year late.

The cutover day does not proceed as planned. The limited distance of stage one deployment results in a massive number of commuters from buses arriving at a transit station a short way outside downtown. The number of commuters waiting at the stations increases due to rail car breakdowns. Some commuters become unhappy with delays, and when the rail cars arrive, they force the doors open so everyone can enter, causing the doors to break and incurring further delays. The following days and weeks do not improve as some rail cars experience broken axles and leave the track. The frequency of breakdowns results in reinstituting bus routes since it is rare to have all trains running during peak times.

1. How can AI algorithms be trained to forecast and respond to political instability in the context of the light rail project? What specific indicators or historical data would be crucial for making accurate predictions?

2. How might AI that uses NLP assist in identifying potential collaboration challenges and ensuring optimal vendor synergy?

3. Consider the unique risks associated with the light rail project and discuss how AI-driven risk management models can identify and address these challenges more effectively.

4. Evaluate the benefits and challenges of implementing an AI-powered system for real time budget monitoring in the light rail deployment. How can such a system prevent overspending, and what specific data points should be considered?

5. What specific historical data, weather patterns, and external factors are crucial for accurate schedule predictions?

6. Given the complexities of the light rail project, discuss how project managers can effectively balance insights from AI algorithms with human expertise in decision-making. What decisions would benefit most from a combination of AI and human judgment?

# PART V

# ACQUIRING AI SOLUTIONS

Organizations have an option to create their own AI-based software or procure it from a vendor. This section starts with an assessment of both options. If an organization does not have the technical ability, the decision to procure becomes easier. Regardless, the organization must understand how AI works and can contribute to improving project performance. The analysis is similar to a business case that evaluates the costs and benefits of procuring AI solutions or developing them internally. Once issues are identified, evaluating vendor solutions typically requires a demo of the software capability and how the proposed solution achieves the benefit. The final chapter in this section discusses the process and pitfalls of implementing AI-based software for project management.

# CHAPTER 15

# THE BUILD OR BUY DECISION

There are advantages and disadvantages to building solutions internally or procuring them from a vendor. Creating software internally brings knowledge to the organization, allowing flexibility and quicker turnaround than the vendor process. Finding skilled resources, especially data scientists and machine learning programmers, might be difficult. Both skillsets command a high level of compensation, and when these workers leave, they take away considerable organizational knowledge. Vendors provide the expertise gained from numerous deployments, making the process easier and faster. Unfortunately, some vendors might be more interested in collecting organizational project data to build general project models for several customers, and this objective might detract from building models that optimize each organization's project performance. Finding the best vendor for your business is critical because your organization will depend on them as updates and changes occur.

TABLE 15.1 Advantages of creating or purchasing an AI solution

| Advantages of Creating AI Internally | Advantages of Purchasing AI |
| --- | --- |
| Increases internal knowledge | Capitalizes on vendor experience |
| Easier to maintain data security | Utilizes standard industry solutions |
| Provides flexibility | Reduces internal resource requirements |
| Allows instant feedback and adjustments | Encourages a focus on data, not algorithms |

One problem with buying from vendors is that each vendor may only have a solution to a specific problem, resulting in a disparate jigsaw puzzle of isolated pieces that may or may not eventually fit together.

AI-based software provides a way to improve the accuracy of project costs, maintain the end date for a schedule, or classify risks. These are all targeted in a specific area, and the problem is that there is no consideration for the overall perspective of the project methodology. AI solutions need to have an integrated perspective in the same way that we expect a project manager to take that responsibility. Having specific software is not necessarily a problem but can eventually result in outcomes that are not tied to the overall benefit of the project. In a situation where there are many projects in an organization, the AI-based solution must also analyze interdependencies and avoid any negative impact on the overall portfolio.

Acquiring a software solution from a vendor requires answers to specific questions. Will the organization be responsible for providing all the structured data, or will the vendor provide guidance and assistance? The level of vendor support is important, as the data determines the accuracy of the machine learning algorithms. Without proper data, the results will be useless. The organization must seek answers using the amount of data required to achieve accurate results, the acceptable level of balanced data, the expected hidden bias in the data, the learning approach used, and how to manage it all. In addition, if the vendor does not have the capability, there might be an organizational requirement to create interfaces for other systems to acquire and use more real time data. A machine learning solution should not be created from a single acquisition of data and then ignored. Using ongoing data to provide continuous updates is more important in a project environment, especially in an organization with many projects or projects with short durations.

Sometimes, the organization can purchase AI software from a vendor and manage the installation and usage within its internal capability. In this situation, the vendor provides instructions and guidance and allows the organization to handle any support they require or want to perform. This is common with organizations using generative AI, where they subscribe to a level of capability and then restrict the analysis and responses to their own database. Some organizations prefer to create all the machine learning algorithms themselves with the help of internal technical resources. A reasonable understanding of the objectives must be achieved before the model is created. Some vendors are very reliable, so it can be tempting to utilize the skills of a familiar company and let them manage the AI software deployment. AI technology is a different skill set and requires new knowledge. It will be difficult to distinguish between capable vendors and those who only want to sell their software unless project managers know how the technology functions. The organization needs to carefully consider the offering and verify that it is a good fit and provides value. The most important consideration, of course, is the data. Assuming that the organization has data, the next question is: Who is responsible for upgrading the data to a structured format that the AI software can use? Even competent vendors will be reluctant to perform this, especially if the organization wants to quickly succeed without acknowledging the poor condition of its data.

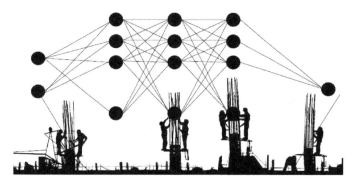

**FIGURE 15.1** Constructing a neural network

As Figure 15.1 demonstrates, building an AI solution can be complex. If an organization decides to create its own machine-learning algorithms, cloud-based platforms can be used to accelerate deployment. Most software vendors use subscriber-based pricing, where payment depends on the business's usage or size. The platforms easily adapt to increased usage as the organization develops and expands. This assumes that the organization has qualified internal skills to create models. Although the platform providers make it sound simple, there needs to be statistical analysis expertise and technical capability to understand the creation and use of machine learning code. The scenario requiring the most internal resources is when the organization creates machine learning algorithms using its own hardware and software resources. The benefit is having resources who understand the organization and are flexible in achieving specific goals. Another advantage is that the process can emphasize the importance of data retention and data management, specifically for project management data. The disadvantage is the requirement to maintain and constantly upgrade hardware and software platforms.

Project managers realize that a reasonable plan is the basis for successfully implementing a project, and acquiring AI solutions is no different. Building a new machine learning algorithm might be fascinating and provide value, but the software will be ineffective if the data does not exist. The project manager needs to consider the objectives for applying AI-based solutions to the project methodology. Regardless of the decision, the organization must successfully implement the AI solution and evaluate if the results provide the expected value.

## RESOURCES TO CREATE AI SOFTWARE FOR PROJECT MANAGEMENT

Once an idea for using AI for project management is identified, the software must be created. There are some resources that help create or manage software algorithms. It is impossible to find and list them all, but a sample selection can help organizations understand what types of external resources are available.

### Fiverr

Fiverr is one of many freelance services that allows clients to create a scope statement for the service they want and have qualified bidders attempt to win the contract. Workers with technical skills can be hired to develop machine learning programs or NLP applications.

*www.fiverr.com*

### Gigster

Gigster offers coding services, especially for entrepreneurs or start-ups, and the company has workers with AI expertise. AI development is typically a higher-priced option with a focus that includes enterprise software solutions.

*www.gigster.com*

## Kaggle

The Kaggle web site is home to a community of data scientists and others who share ideas and results, and has contests in machine learning. Data scientists can earn extra money or gain more knowledge by participating in their spare time. The competitions are real and life-changing, like the machine learning competition to detect pneumothorax disease based on chest x-ray images. The outcome of the competition for a $30,000 prize was to use AI software to triage authentic images for priority attention and to increase confidence in the correct diagnosis. A machine learning algorithm performed better than technicians in analyzing these challenging images. Google owns the site and offers free courses in machine learning topics such as Python programming and data visualization.

*kaggle.com*

## Github

GitHub is an open source repository where programmers store and access software code in a controlled manner. It offers good version control, and users can access their section with a unique URL. It is frequently used as a reference source for online programming courses or books that refer to lines of code that can be accessed for practice, which is how many programmers discover it. It handles both private and public projects.

*github.com*

## Stack Overflow

Stack Overflow allows software developers to ask questions and receive answers from other programmers. It is an open community offering private and public forums for solving coding problems. In addition, it offers a job listing section.

*stackoverflow.com*

## Neural Network Playground

Neural Network Playground is a Google-sponsored Web site that allows users to build and test a simple neural network used for classification. It provides an overview of components, allows a selection, and gives a real time visual display of how the neural network works to classify the data.

*playground.tensorflow.org*

Project management is a business segment that needs to adopt more technology. There are numerous options for project scheduling software. Other software, such as checking documents for accurate content or verifying consistency in a project plan, were developed as general business software and adopted by project managers. Given the importance and scale of projects being implemented worldwide, it is surprising that many people consider project management to be a "manual" exercise. Organizations want to have a successful project but are unsure of the most effective methodology to deliver a successful project. It will be interesting to discover if a single software system can increase project success rates or whether the software will be customized for specific project types or industries. It will also be interesting to see if large software companies such as Google or Microsoft become more involved in creating AI software specifically for project management. With the gig economy, it is much easier for small businesses to develop software. The numerous vendors offering project scheduling software may attempt to alter their software to include machine learning algorithms.

## QUESTIONS

### Review questions

1. What are the critical aspects to consider before building or buying an AI-based solution?

2. What difficulties can be expected when developing AI capacity internally?

3. What difficulties can be expected when acquiring AI software from a vendor?

### Discussion questions

1. How can an organization determine if it is best to build or buy AI software algorithms?

2. Does a build or buy decision change how the organization communicates the decision to stakeholders?

# CHAPTER 16

# *EVALUATING AND ACQUIRING AI SOFTWARE*

R esearch suggests that machine learning will drive profound economic changes in the world and people's lives (Agrawal, Gans,
and Goldfarb 2022). As machine learning algorithms and the
accompanying infrastructure become less costly, the usage will increase.
Everything from everyday decision-making to complex strategy development will become more effective due to machine learning, resulting
in an economic improvement. How can a project manager take advantage of the dramatically lower cost of machine learning algorithms?
The most effective approach is to redesign the processes for managing
projects and then find efficiencies within those processes. Improved
efficiency is possible in all areas of project management. Aside from
any incremental benefits, there is a need to adopt the most effective
software for a specific organization or type of project. Strategic decisions are required to determine whether to improve existing processes
or completely redefine the processes. As more AI capability becomes
available for project management, an evaluation is needed before a
decision is made to acquire AI-based software.

Many AI programs are free to use with limited capability, and most
companies offer a subscription service for additional features. This is a
way to learn how the software is used and reduces the risk. Three basic
concepts should be considered when implementing an AI solution for
project management:

- optimization of AI value

- consideration of an integrated approach

- development of ubiquitous project management

The first part of this approach is to maximize value, and since AI is a disruptive technology, the most significant value should involve a disruption to the current project management methodology. Simply stated, the software should change how projects are initiated, planned, and deployed. AI capability is implemented somewhere in the process, and it needs to return significant value compared to the costs. This approach also means that a project manager must ensure that project management changes are correctly implemented, and that this is done in an integrated or holistic manner. Project managers are responsible for taking an overall perspective of the project, and with each team member concentrating on specific assigned tasks, it is often only the project manager who has the total view of the project. With that in mind, the AI software should find a way to consider all aspects of the project. In other words, the AI solution should not increase quality yet have the side effect of increasing risk. The new capability should not optimize resources if that means reducing quality. These trade-offs deliver lower value, and the project manager may need help explaining and managing the adverse and unexpected side effects. Finally, ubiquitous project management is the ability to manage a project from anywhere at any time. Using voice commands to interact with AI will become pervasive. Although this might be a more accessible management style for some people, the objective is to access accurate project data and make effective project decisions. Whether a project manager performs the work from a smartphone or laptop, the supporting capability must be based on an integrated view of all the project's moving parts. The decisions require logic that is applied correctly to resolve project issues. The project manager cannot make good decisions or communicate effectively if there are gaps in the data or negative repercussions that are not considered.

These concepts are important to consider in light of the various AI capabilities that are being offered to project managers and PMOs. Some AI-based software will provide value, and some will be useless. There needs to be a good fit for the organization, and the solution must improve the project process. Understanding how these three concepts function will hopefully steer purchasing decisions in the right direction.

As AI solutions for project management are developed and become competitive, so will the sales pitches. Project managers need to be wary of unrealistic offers, such as those made without a comprehensive understanding of the manager's needs and goals. Software vendors may make unrealistic offers in order to sell their products. Technical details, such as what training algorithm is used and how to avoid hidden bias in the data, should be taken into consideration when purchasing software. AI-based software may seen as useful, but project managers must understand how the logic engine works. Do not be afraid to ask questions about how the technology operates. Some questions to ask are as follows:

- What technology is used: SVM, random forest, Naive Bayes, or a neural network?

- What is the expected level of hidden bias, and how can it be minimized or eliminated?

- How much and what type of data is required to deliver accurate results?

These questions help determine whether this is a machine learning-based algorithm or an expert system with many rules and predetermined responses. If unsure, seek help from an expert before spending a large sum of money on an AI system.

## STRATEGY FOR IMPLEMENTING AI

Numerous AI software solutions for project management are now available, and more are being developed. Decisions will be made about which software program to acquire and what software is the best fit for the organization. AI technology development is progressing rapidly, and the impact on project management will be profound. How can project managers make good decisions with the onset of AI proliferation? The first step in any strategy is to gain knowledge and become more educated and aware of the technology.

Some recommended strategies are as follows:

- Investigate how the software and data requirements for AI-based software fit into the existing technical infrastructure.

- Decide what capability provides the greatest value in the project management process. What is the greatest pain: cost overrun, late due dates, resource availability, or another source of trouble?

- Develop a good business case for purchasing and implementing AI technology.

- Recognize the value of project data and set standards for nomenclature, data maintenance, and data retention.

- Set clear policies and procedures to oversee the acquisition of AI technology for project management.

- Encourage pilot projects to test the effectiveness of AI solutions. This is an excellent way to increase knowledge and discover value early.

- If the organization is risk averse, follow the industry. The organization does not have to be a leader in adopting AI for project management, but it should not be willing to fall too far behind.

- Assess what works and then select the best solutions.

- Actively seek collaboration with similar organizations and promote knowledge-sharing opportunities.

- Find a partner who understands how to use AI software.

- Ensure project managers are trained in AI fundamentals, including managing data and interpreting machine learning results.

Which organizations will gain the most from AI, and which organizations will feel pain and subsequently be left behind in adopting new technology? The most obvious winner will be larger organizations that have a lot of accessible project data that can be used for data mining to discover anomalies or for machine learning algorithms to discover patterns of success or failure. Once these organizations benefit from the value of machine learning software for project management, they will likely see a virtuous improvement cycle. They maintain good data habits, find more interesting ways to improve their project methodology, and accelerate their determination to store structured and accessible project data.

Smaller organizations and associations with very little data to use will suffer the impact of being unable to monetize any value from project data. They need to find a collaborative approach or hope that preprogrammed machine learning software from a vendor or contracted company will apply to their projects, which is uncertain. Project managers who accept AI technology and understand the limitations and opportunities will be in demand by organizations seeking a competitive edge. Knowledgeable project managers will know what the results produced by AI software mean and find ways to use the results to increase project performance.

There will always be stakeholders who fear new technology and refuse to change. Stakeholders must find a way to accept AI technology and take advantage of what is offered. Project managers and other stakeholders must also be patient because adopting new technology can be challenging. Problems arise that need to be resolved. Training is required to understand how to use and optimize the latest technology, but the reward is worth it. One of the benefits of machine learning is that, given enough data, the results will be automatically customized to the specific organization rather than generic. Some conditions or circumstances may be similar to projects implemented in other organizations, but an organization's culture and processes are usually unique. This uniqueness can be reflected in the algorithm training process and used to make predictions or classifications that increase project management success rates.

## QUESTIONS

### Review questions

1. What value is achieved by acquiring AI software from a vendor?

2. What are the pitfalls of acquiring AI software for project management?

### Discussion questions

1. Will the implementation process for acquiring AI software solutions be different for different organizations?

2. How does an organization ensure that the benefit of acquiring AI technology for project management outweighs the costs?

## REFERENCES

Agrawal, A., Gans, J., and Goldfarb, A. (2022). *Power and prediction: The disruptive economics of artificial intelligence*. Harvard Business Review Press.

## CASE STUDY: VENDOR SELECTION

A consultant was hired for a nonprofit association that did not have project management experience. The organization desperately needed to improve customer service and promptly manage activities with stakeholders. An AI-based customer relationship management software solution was requested from vendors, and a request for proposal (RFP) to acquire and deploy it was issued. A senior manager for the association scored the financial submissions worth 30 percent of the total score, and a project management consultant scored the nonfinancial criteria worth the remaining 70 percent. One vendor was ranked at the bottom of the nonfinancial factors, so the consultant was surprised to see that they were listed in the top three granted meetings to convince the organization that they should be selected.

The vendor ranking lowest on nonfinancial factors submitted the lowest financial bid and won the contract. At one of the first meetings, the contractor's project manager for the software deployment outlined a questionable process and vague plans for the deployment. A revolving door of four different project managers was assigned over the first year. Quality and risk issues were never taken seriously, which only confirmed the evaluation results on nonfinancial issues. On the financial side, they overspent all estimates and tried various ways to explain it. The cost overruns had to be paid for by the association to keep the project moving. The vendor selected had little AI training and no consistent project methodology to deploy the solution. After years of overspending and project delays, the software was implemented. The organization faces an ongoing challenge to utilize the software effectively.

1. Did the factors in the RFQ represent the project objectives?

2. Was the result predictable, and what could have been done to avoid it?

3. What factors help detect a poor implementation process or project plan?

# CHAPTER 17

# *IMPLEMENTING AI SOLUTIONS*

Here is a suggested step-by-step approach for how to improve the current project processes with AI software. This is a rather generic description, and project managers must select specific solutions that will have an impact.

1. Gather metrics regarding the current project success rates and project performance. This includes whether projects delivered the original project scope and any variances to budget and schedule. It can consist of any penalties or losses incurred from the project, which can be used as part of the business case. Identify any waste or inefficiencies that hurt the value of the organization.

2. Document the existing project methodology used by the organization. An honest appraisal is an important step. If there are no clear standards and no consistent process, it is still valuable to capture that variability. Identify the metrics for how projects are tracked, and results are reported. This step is meant to help with understanding how the process will change. There can be both disruptive solutions that change the methodology and task efficiency software, as long as the task efficiency software does not prevent the methodology from changing when new technology is added.

3. Verify that the project data is structured, available, and accessible.

4. Build the business case for making changes to the project processes. This should be straightforward for project managers who

want to improve the project success rate, and quantifying the benefits should be an inspirational event.

5. Start a project that can be used to test the new technology and verify its value. This needs to be part of a broader change management process. Change management is a significant factor in implementing new technology successfully.

6. Evaluate the results against the business case and the metrics collected about current success rates.

7. Incorporate the changes into the new project methodology for all projects.

These suggestions provide a foundation for developing an implementation strategy. Each organization may differ based on size, type, culture, and other factors. Every step might seem too slow, but keep the objective in mind. The goal is to take project success rates and performance to unprecedented levels.

One of the most significant project areas to improve is risk management. For the projects being initiated, the change to a new method should not result in decreased project performance and a lower success rate. Like the Hippocratic oath for doctors, AI should at least "do no harm." A deterioration in the process leads to fear of implementing change, which is rarely a useful strategy. It takes commitment and courage to move forward with an improvement plan. As long as the knowledge and understanding are acquired, deploying AI has a high probability of improving the process. Some organizations fail to successfully deploy machine learning software. Ineffective deployment can create negative sentiment. The chances of increasing project performance are low if there is no solid business case, clear objectives, or strategy for deploying AI.

There is always a possibility that some stakeholders will deliberately attempt to sabotage changes. All software is vulnerable, although project management seems less likely than most to become infiltrated and misused. For a highly visible project, the easiest way to sabotage it is to provide corrupt input data that makes the prediction and classification unreliable. This is a warning to keep the data safe and protected, which should be in effect regardless of using AI software. Despite the obstacles, there is a clear path to implementing AI solutions to improve project success rates. The strategy and steps outlined in this section make implementation easier.

## THE AI ROADMAP

From a PMO perspective, or simply for an organization looking to implement machine learning and NLP, it is no different from other technology in that it needs a roadmap. Determine the strategy for implementing AI into the project methodology to guarantee a success rate of 95 percent or higher. The first step is to define the scope and boundaries, which includes setting a time frame for creating the vision that will result in implementing AI solutions. The next step is to assess what software is a good fit for the project processes based on the new methodology. This also requires a review of the system requirements since machine learning algorithms need data. The roadmap will likely include other capabilities the organization plans to implement based on system design. The final part is to review and critique the roadmap to ensure it is sound and robust.

The scope review for the roadmap includes an analysis of how the project processes need to be changed or improved. Based on changes, the organization might need better data management, a different mix of Agile and waterfall processes, or more project management training. There needs to be a clearly identified objective for implementing AI. Data mining can be used to look for correlations, but creating an objective for data mining is required before beginning the work. This applies to machine learning, as well. Implementing a change starts with defining the objective for what is to be accomplished. Then, a strategy is created, such as finding and accessing the data, building a machine learning algorithm, training the software, and predicting or classifying a new dataset. If the outcome does not align with the purpose, the process starts again.

If the organization has uncertainty over AI for project management, there needs to be a decision around a proof of concept, initial trial, or full-blown implementation. One of the frequently used techniques in project management is using a project management expert. This refers to someone who has experience on many projects and is likely to have more information than someone new to the project team. The opportunity for a project manager is to become a new subject-matter expert in AI-based project software. AI brings new approaches to planning projects, delivering projects, and making decisions to solve project issues. A project manager can learn about AI software that utilizes available historical information to determine the best plans and strategy.

For many software deployments use cases are developed first. These are problems or opportunities to use software to create a solution. What problems need to be solved in managing projects, and how can they be solved using a machine learning algorithm? This might result in a piecemeal approach to changing the project management process. The goal should be to disrupt the process to consistently achieve significantly higher project success rates. The second part is to review all AI solutions available and decide what to implement. Identify the software that provides the most benefit, both short term and long-term. Although machine learning algorithms are powerful, they become even more effective when integrated with other technologies. For example, the Internet of Things (IoT) technology includes sensors capable of informing the project manager when a task is complete. Some types of AI software have an imaging capability to capture a snapshot of a building under construction and determine what percentage of the work is complete. AI can detect quality issues or defects and match both to the expected values at this stage of the project. A prediction algorithm is an excellent example of software that can be integrated into numerous project management requirements, such as scheduling, resource allocation, risk planning, and budgeting. For each of these, a prediction is made as to the probability of success of the project based on the plan in place or the status of each deliverable as the project is underway. In this situation, a requirements traceability matrix is useful. Machine learning software understands each requirement and the work necessary to achieve it. As the project progresses and resource shortages or budget reductions occur, the software can suggest appropriate trade-offs on objectives. The highest value objective can be achieved, while the lower value objectives may be deferred or delivered later. AI can place a value on each objective and ensure that they are still valid and achievable as the project progresses toward the goal.

Of course, it costs money to implement new technology, and most providers offer a free trial that allows users to appreciate the value before realizing that the AI solution is indispensable. This is followed by a subscription-based payment model. The danger in using this approach is that the organization selects the easiest solution to implement with a good return. This strategy is used frequently in organizations, and it causes two problems. When organizations pick the "easy wins," stakeholders are misled into believing all changes will be easy. The reality is that further changes are much more difficult yet might deliver far greater value. Second, it encourages a piecemeal approach to improving a process. Project managers should strive for the most significant gains in project success rates. The best plan is a comprehensive approach to changing the project methodology. If project management is at the heart of the organization's success, keeping the big picture in mind and disrupting the project management processes is essential.

The final step in a roadmap or strategy for AI software implementation is to keep it current. This applies to both the software and the data. After successfully implementing the software, a plan is required to stay current. Creating a strategy to implement AI has three steps.

1. Decide where the organization wants to be in terms of project performance.

2. Decide what the project processes and results are needed now.

3. Create a plan to reach each goal.

The most challenging part for many people and organizations is understanding the existing project methodology. That will likely be a big challenge for organizations that want to implement AI for project management. Understanding the current state is not only about technical competence and preparedness but also about culture and the desire to create and implement a plan for improvements. That plan may include more changes to the current state than organizations realize. Initial work with AI may be encouraging, but it will take experience and perseverance to achieve project success rates that are significantly higher than today. In some instances, AI will be implemented poorly. Sometimes, the data is insufficient or contains corrupt values, leading to incorrect results and predictions. Another problem is that expertise is limited in how AI can and should be applied to project management. It will also take a mindset change. Organizations need a champion to promote the potential of AI technology, and they also need a project manager who can work with data to discover an ideal time and place to start and then show improved results.

The selection and implementation of AI requires a structured approach based on a plan of how the AI software will increase project success rates. The strategy begins with understanding the existing project process and formulating a strategy to make changes. The cost of developing and implementing AI software is constantly decreasing, which will result in a greater variety of options for project management. The selection of AI software needs to consider several factors, such as the benefit to the organization and the ability to radically change the existing project methodology.

## QUESTIONS

### Review questions

1. Describe an implementation process that is likely to be successful

2. How can an organization reduce the risk of acquiring AI technology?

### Discussion questions

1. How can vendor claims be verified?

2. What factors determine which vendor software will provide the greatest value?

3. What are the similarities and differences for a project to implement AI-based software that changes the organization's project methodology?

## CASE STUDY: DEPLOYMENT ISSUES

A project manager works for an organization with large-scale manufacturing software deployed on-site that is essential for correctly processing products within quality limits. The organization believes in continuous improvement and is willing to utilize new technology. After speaking with some stakeholders, the project manager creates a business case for new AI-based software and, through persuasiveness with senior management, receives approval to spend over $200,000 on the new software. The project manager moves to another role and, a few years later, meets the team assigned to implement the new software. The project manager was told that the implementation was stopped because none of the new software capabilities delivered the expected results. In addition, implementation was complicated, and the users had other priorities. As a result, the organization stopped the further evaluation of AI software.

1. What factors should have been considered before acquiring the new software?

2. Is there a different strategy that might have worked to implement the software?

3. How does this result impact the future deployment of AI-based software?

# PART VI

# ADAPTING TO AI IN PROJECT MANAGEMENT

Since the transition to using AI in project management is inevitable, it is worthwhile to consider the implications. The most noticeable factor for successfully deploying AI to change the project methodology will be a change in the roles of project practitioners. Project managers are at the forefront of this change, but PMO staff and the project team will also have different responsibilities. The focus is on how each participant contributes to success.

The second area reviewed in this section is an example of one responsibility that is unavoidable. Concerns about the ethical use of AI are important to understand. With AI, new considerations need attention from project managers. AI requires vigilance beyond managing data privacy. Monitoring and managing ethical issues will be a challenge for project management. A survey of ethical concerns and potential remediation is included to help project managers understand the impending situation.

The final area reviewed is technology beyond AI and how it will drive the next wave of project process improvements. The most likely development will be a combination of AI and other technologies to create more powerful and intelligent solutions. Project managers are responsible for adapting to and embracing the right changes at the most advantageous time for the organization.

CHAPTER 18

# CHANGES TO ROLES OF THE PROJECT MANAGER, PMO, AND PROJECT TEAM

T he most significant changes are to those who plan and deliver a project: project managers, the PMO, and the project team.

## PROJECT MANAGERS

Projects create change in society, and it is a project manager's responsibility to implement these changes successfully. With the introduction of AI technology, the project manager's role will change. The responsibilities of a project manager will be different, and the way projects are delivered will change. Preparing for the changes wrought by AI technology is difficult because many project managers have little insight into the changes and how to adapt. In addition to being the drivers of change in the environment, project managers will be the recipients of changes to their own roles. Project managers must be prepared for this change.

Change management includes aspects of communication, training, and process redesign. These are the main items that need to be addressed for project managers who are faced with adopting AI technology. Communication is used to alleviate fears and provide an explanation of changes. Training is required to ensure that the new technology is used properly. Process redesign will involve determining and deploying a new way to perform project management. The changes to the role of a project manager will occur in stages. In the short term, the project manager needs to understand the new technology, find its value, implement it properly, and collaborate with AI software to achieve better project results. This can only be accomplished by using change management skills. The big issue with changes due to AI is that the new technology has an impact on both project management processes and how project practitioners perform their work. For now, adopting AI requires a project manager to understand the interaction between data and the software used to support good project management decisions. Generative AI delivers significant productivity gains, but the output needs to be verified. Becoming too reliant on AI is a risk. How will project managers react to receiving instructions and direction from a software program? It may be an improvement for some because it aligns with their determination to succeed. Some projects will require the project manager to spend more time managing accurate and consistent data flows than making decisions to manage the project. This will be the longest stage in this transition to AI software for project management. Eventually, as AI software has more data, is more easily trained, and adapts to the organizational environment, it becomes easier for the project manager to work cohesively with AI technology as part of the project methodology. With success, the project manager may be able to manage many more projects simultaneously. For project managers who already feel overloaded, increasing their workload may not be a good strategy. The final stage of project process improvement might be much like Geoffrey Hinton's belief that AI can do anything a human can (Peng 2019). This presumes the eventual result is a self-directed project.

At some point in the future, AI technology will make all the same project management decisions as a project manager. In that situation, the project manager can be elevated to a PMO level where the project manager oversees numerous projects simultaneously. For some people, this is inaccurate, and when articles are published with content similar to this, the feedback usually contains reasons why a machine can never replace a project manager. This is an indication that there will be resistance to change. Project managers cannot delay the advance of technology, so they are obligated to make it work. There will be a period of time with failures, and those against using AI software in project management will point at those failures as proof of the inadequacy of AI-based solutions. Continued project failure rates will increase the urgency to replace project manager functions. AI algorithms detect correlations beyond human capability. They perform faster and can analyze far more variables than a project manager. Comprehensive and quick analysis will become essential, especially with large and complex projects. Sponsors and customers will demand higher project success rates that can only be achieved by using AI technology. In a recent study of diagnosing tumors from brain scans, doctors were accurate in 66 percent of the cases, and an AI program was correct 83 percent of the time (Yamei 2018). This is not surprising considering AI software's advanced image recognition capability. The success rate can be increased if the two work together, which is a lesson for project managers. Working collaboratively with AI improves project success.

## THE PROJECT MANAGEMENT OFFICE

For organizations that have one, the PMO will be responsible for deploying AI to change the project methodology and ensure that the changes are followed. Patience is required when learning from initial failures. Metrics are more critical at every stage of the project because trends are monitored more closely and become part of the data required by machine learning algorithms. The PMO also needs metrics that demonstrate the success of the new methodology and show gains made by implementing AI-based processes. The PMO is responsible for auditing to ensure that AI systems conform to standard practices and meet employee and societal expectations, especially regarding ethics and privacy.

PMO staff will continue to initiate, manage, and monitor projects, but with AI, they now have a new and powerful advantage. AI not only improves the project processes but will also provide PMO staff with advanced and marketable skills in managing data and understanding the strategic value of AI software. The PMO must become more comfortable with math and statistics, especially regression analysis. There is a learning curve as AI software is adopted, and increased training is required to achieve optimal results. In addition, the PMO must take control of project data management. This is a significant role considering the time required to manage data for the first deployment of AI. With this knowledge and an understanding of the advantages and pitfalls of the new AI software, the PMO needs to identify the training required for all project staff.

A significant challenge faced by some PMOs is to demonstrate that having a PMO provides value to the organization on an ongoing basis. Using AI offers numerous possibilities to make this claim. A measurable example is the ability to deliver the project successfully at a lower cost. The lower cost is achieved using generative AI for productivity improvements and machine learning algorithms for technical decision-making and optimizing resources. The existence of a PMO is justified by their ability to continue to assess and implement AI software that improves the project methodology, thereby providing increased value to the organization. The new PMO must rely less on existing software and embrace machine learning algorithms and other AI capabilities. The PMO must facilitate the ability for projects to use an integrated approach within a specific project and across all projects in the program or portfolio. This is essential for project-based organizations. By focusing on data and making good decisions based on data, machine learning algorithms reduce the complexity of projects. The PMO must identify the most cost-effective projects and analyze the reasons and conditions that result in the cost-effective results. The objective is to replicate that set of conditions for other projects. The PMO can push the organization's capability and find ways to use the existing methodology for more challenging projects.

Larger, geographically dispersed, or more technologically complex projects can be completed because the new AI-influenced methodology is a competitive advantage. The PMO may become an expert at managing an AI-infused process and offer advice on achieving success.

To properly facilitate the success of the PMO, there must be a vigorous effort to manage project data, which plays a central role in obtaining useful results from AI software. The PMO needs to identify portfolio data, which may be useful for AI utilization at the PMO's level. For example, a dashboard of project metrics from several projects can be analyzed for trends and possible negative project interactions. A new PMO dashboard must contain machine learning outcomes, such as the prediction of project success, as well as schedule and cost projections based on historical data. The PMO needs to evaluate what machine learning algorithms are working the best and which ones must be revised or updated. Machine learning is unlike programs that are coded using a set of rules where there is either a correct answer or no answer at all. Machine learning builds a model that represents the project management data. The outcome of an algorithm might not produce a perfectly reliable result. Like other metrics, the PMO can develop guidelines on how the outcomes can be used. A result does not have to be perfect for decision-making but must be properly understood. Perhaps the project needs to make further progress before providing more data for the algorithm to be more accurate. Another consideration is identifying which machine learning methods are being used for prediction. A neural network is commonly used, although there are times when other prediction methods, such as SVM, random forest, or Naive Bayes, are also helpful. The organization may have some unique attribute that makes one type of algorithm inherently more successful than others. This is an area where technical collaboration is essential, although it is better for the PMO to have this responsibility because they have a better overall organizational perspective.

With a new AI-based project methodology, the PMO becomes the caretaker of data and the learning process for using machine learning algorithms. They can produce new policies and procedures for each project manager to follow. Still, the PMO needs to monitor adherence, as any lapse in proper data management can reduce the value of a machine learning outcome. The new PMO will also have a role in managing stakeholders and communicating with them. There are, of course, concerns regarding data privacy and ethical considerations. Data is becoming more valuable due to machine learning software because data is the nutrient that feeds the machine learning algorithms. Data security is critical for organizations that have sufficient historical project data, especially where the algorithms produce consistently good results. To clearly understand the results being produced, the PMO staff needs additional training in statistics because that is the basis for building machine learning models. Using the results can be invasive, depending on how aggressive the organization wants to be when taking advantage of all the capabilities of AI software. Stakeholder habits and communications can be analyzed to build psychological profiles, and these profiles can then be used to manage the project stakeholders. The PMO may be the "gatekeeper" who determines the level of monitoring that is considered too invasive.

The PMO needs more input on how project managers are hired, the way that project managers are trained, and which project managers are assigned to specific projects. As the project methodology evolves, project manager training must move away from training for communication and leadership skills and toward managing data appropriately, understanding the mathematical results produced by AI software, and how to interpret and best utilize AI results. Formal training in communication skills is a lesser priority because AI software can be used to coach the project manager on optimizing communication. AI software can also effectively motivate, persuade, and console stakeholders individually, depending on their personality profile and emotional state. Project managers need a strong background in math and statistics to understand how the data fed to the machine learning algorithms is used to identify correlations.

Machine learning algorithms can effectively analyze data, but humans must manage the results and interpret the best way to move forward with the project. AI has difficulty with abstraction. The project manager uses a higher-level understanding to implement machine learning results, and so the PMO will need to rethink how project managers are assigned to projects. Projects that require more effective communication with fragile stakeholders do not necessarily need to be assigned to a project manager who has the most training in interpersonal skills. Instead, this project can be assigned to a project manager who has demonstrated capability in implementing machine learning results and uses personality profiles combined with AI suggestions to communicate to stakeholders. A smaller project where there is possibly less data to feed AI software can be assigned to a project manager who is more skilled at managing on their own. To help AI software be more effective with similar projects in the future, the project manager can then search for ways to gather more data from similar projects. In the near future, the assignments of project managers will change and will no longer be based on typical skills and experience. The PMO must build expertise in this new matrix of matching the best project managers or project teams to projects.

Project resources will also have new criteria for being allocated to a project. It might not be based on who is free or available at a given time. The new allocation is based on who is the best fit for each project when considering the entire portfolio of projects in the organization. Similarly, allocating funds for internal projects might be based on advancing the project methodology, the ability to implement a lean project with the highest probability of success, and the project most aligned with the organization's goals. The role of the PMO will expand to include much more interaction with other functional groups. The PMO in a project-based organization controls the knowledge needed to make the best decisions in different functional areas. For example, with human resources staff, the PMO will recommend the new skill set required for project managers and project team members. When interacting with an IT group, the PMO will indicate the need for an effective data strategy and how to maintain and improve machine learning algorithms. For external vendors contracted through a procurement department, the PMO becomes a consultant to determine whether the vendors have and plan to deploy AI software. The PMO determines whether the AI software will be effective for the work required and whether the software enhances the ability to deliver the full scope of the project on time and within budget. The PMO can require that vendors provide evidence of the effectiveness of their machine learning algorithms. They can ask about their AI methodology, hidden bias, and the data strategy that makes them a better choice than alternative vendors.

Another potential role for the PMO is to help develop the integrated technical approach with other software in the digital transformation portfolio, such as sensor or blockchain technology. The power of AI software can be increased by combining it with other technology, but a sensible strategy needs to be developed. Sensor technology can detect changes and be used to identify the status of various activities in a project automatically. Using this technology also means a considerable volume of additional data, especially streaming data, which will be available about the project and must be appropriately managed. The PMO must be able to use digital technology to manage projects and a portfolio more effectively. Digital sensors can be set up to share with other projects to track or optimize the dependencies. The PMO can help determine where different technologies should be deployed to provide valuable information on projects.

## PROJECT TEAM

The objective for project team members is to complete their assigned tasks on the project. Although this can be an individual responsibility, there are times when collaboration and communication are essential. AI will improve communication and clarify tasks so individuals can accomplish them with greater certainty and efficiency. Alternately, some AI software programs use analytics to suggest removing team members from a task if they are not performing well enough. Replacing individuals on tasks can be a sensitive issue for project teams and may not be well received, especially if the AI software ignores valid personal reasons for the performance. All project managers want high-performing team members in every project and on every task, but that is not feasible. Sometimes, the assignments must be the best fit for employees and tasks. That may not optimize each task, although it can optimize the project work as a whole.

Project team members have a significant role in implementing AI software. They are an excellent source for finding data that can be used for input to machine learning software. They also need to be motivated and accept the changes in the project methodology for using AI software. This will be important since implementing AI software into project management processes is similar to most new technology and initially may perform poorly. Project team members who understand and work well with the latest technology will be rewarded for their increased knowledge and ability to adapt to the new reality of project processes.

The most intriguing question is whether the project team can be led by AI software instead of a project manager. A globally dispersed project team with employees working remotely may not notice the absence of a project manager. In other situations, the team members may not require interactions with the project manager to complete the assigned tasks. Exceptions such as requesting vacation time or a leave of absence are often handled within self-directed project teams in today's workforce. Indeed, many less critical issues can be resolved with team interaction and not with the intervention of a project manager. Some people will gladly accept AI software if it means less time in meetings. It should be a standard practice to communicate project issues as soon as they occur to allow immediate communication with the proper stakeholders and promote faster resolution. This is also important with an AI-based process, but it raises the question of the project manager's role in projects and which parts of those activities are better performed by AI.

AI will influence the value of certification for project managers and project team members. Certification gives a greater sense that the project member has more knowledge and is more capable of completing project activities. As certification evolves to adopt AI content, it will provide further incentives to receive a credential. The value to consider in using AI for project management will be knowing more about AI technology and its workings. The project manager does not have to be able to write algorithms, but should understand that data is essential and which datasets are being fed into the software.

## TRAINING

Training in AI technology involves employees other than project managers. AI in project management will become pervasive and affect how projects are performed. Project productivity will improve, and project decisions can be made with a higher probability of success. Project practitioners must be aware of this technology's rewards and risks. Successful AI implementation requires a collaborative effort between humans and software. Training and knowledge are critical for that collaboration to be successful. This is a list of essential skills and competencies to be acquired.

1. knowledge of machine learning methods and practical applications

2. knowledge of natural language processing methods and practical applications

3. knowledge of robotic process automation combined with machine learning capability

4. knowledge of statistical methods and the application of regression analysis to data

5. knowledge of data management processes such as structured data entry, data wrangling, and feature engineering

6. knowledge of ethical issues in AI and how to avoid or resolve them

For projects, providing all stakeholders with additional knowledge about AI is beneficial. The training can be segmented by the level of project responsibility in the project or the organization. The project manager plays a critical role. There are three skills project managers need to learn to collaborate successfully with AI software.

**1.** Fundamentals of machine learning and natural language processing

Whether the AI-based solution is provided by a vendor or created internally by programmers, the project manager should understand the fundamental capability of these two components. Machine learning is the engine that drives most but not all AI solutions, including generative AI. A software program uses loops or iterations to refine the correlation performed by regression analysis. Hyperparameters are set before the program begins and include items such as the number of iterations and the number of layers in the neural network. It is essential to ask relevant questions, such as the number of datasets used to make the prediction and, in supervised learning, if the dataset labels are balanced.

NLP uses numerous techniques to interpret language and generate a response. Generative AI, such as a large language model, depends on a corpus or body of work to provide useful responses since the data that is accessed significantly impacts the output. A project manager understands project information and must be involved in how generative AI software accesses and uses project data.

**2.** Data management

AI requires data, and, in most situations, relevant data will be more critical than volumes of data. Data wrangling and feature engineering are necessary for proper input. An information technology worker and a data scientist may not understand the nuances of project data. The project manager is the best person to identify the correct data, relevant data fields, and amount of data required for AI software. The same principle applies to understanding what documents and historical data are most relevant for generative AI processing.

**3.** Math and statistics

AI is based on math: the algorithms use regression analysis to produce results. Statistics is an important component for understanding and interpreting the output. Although a high-level degree in math is not required, project managers must become familiar with managing different aspects of statistical analysis. An example of a situation a project manager may need to address is shown in Figure 18.1. Can the manager ignore the outlier in the data, or is it the start of a new trend?

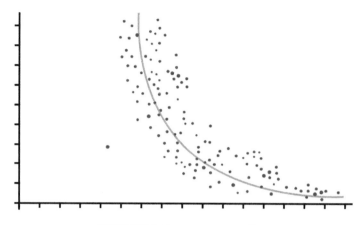

**FIGURE 18.1** How to manage outliers

Project managers have a critical role in adopting and successfully applying AI to improve project performance. There are new areas where training and additional knowledge are essential for this process. Collaborating with AI software allows project managers to demonstrate their value to project stakeholders. Improving these three skills should help project managers and project practitioners strengthen their value to any organization.

## QUESTIONS

### Review questions

1. What are the training requirements for deploying AI successfully?

2. How are the project manager's responsibilities different from the PMO?

3. What role do project team members have when the project is using AI-based software?

### Discussion questions

1. Who has more responsibility to deploy AI, the project manager or the PMO?

2. Can project team members influence how AI is deployed?

3. Will project managers be less likely to deploy AI-based software because their role will change?

4. How does training in each of the three main areas improve a project manager's career opportunities or future advancement?

## REFERENCES

Peng, T. (2019). "Google I/O 2019: Geoffrey Hinton Says Machines Can Do Anything Humans Can," Synched, *https://medium.com/ syncedreview/ google-i-o-2019-geoffrey-hinton-says-machines-can-do-anything-humans-can-460dff834ae2*

Synced. (2019) "Anything Humans Can," Synched, May, 2019, *https:// medium.com/syncedreview/google-i-o-2019-geoffrey-hinton-says-machines-can-do-anything-humans-can-460dff834ae2*

Yamei. (2019). "Chinese AI Beats Human Doctors in Diagnosing Brain Tumours," AI Business, June 30, 2018, *https://aibusiness.com/ chinese-ai-diagnosis-brain-tumours/*

# CHAPTER 19

# ETHICAL IMPLICATIONS OF AI IN PROJECT MANAGEMENT

M any people have misconceptions about AI ethical issues. They are concerned about AI-based systems making serious errors or causing harm. These are valid concerns, but some people tend to make a false assumption that AI software is self-directed. AI software is created by developers, fed data collected by humans, and implemented as part of a project. A standard of ethics must be in place for all organizations, especially those creating and using AI software. The ethics of AI-based decision-making in projects will be based on the data and software solutions implemented.

## AREAS OF ETHICAL CONCERN

### Data

AI programs are based on access to and analysis of historical data. If the organization and past projects include questionable ethical decisions, that is how the AI will be trained. The technology will mimic the organization's culture and bad habits. An evaluation is required to ensure projects meet and exceed ethical data standards.

### Software Development

A programmer or software developer in an organization creates the software. When software is created with a bug or error, the programmer or organization is responsible. The company or the programmer then issues an update to resolve the flaw. With social media, there is increasing global pressure to manage content to meet ethical standards. For ethics in AI software, the same principle applies. The creator of the technology is responsible for the process that allows AI software to make decisions. AI software creators must ensure that ethical standards are included in the products they deliver. Regulations may encourage adherence, but the responsibility remains with the people who implement and manage AI. AI can be invasive depending on how organizations implement it. Some businesses store user data so user habits can be analyzed, and users can be targeted for individual marketing. Organizations acquire user data for marketing by sending out Web crawlers that perform data mining, hide in places such as router software, and capture every personal click to build a profile. Other businesses take user data and train the machine learning algorithm without storing user data.

For project management, the project team and project stakeholders are most vulnerable to privacy concerns. Current algorithms assess how efficient team members are at completing a task and may recommend a replacement based on habitually slower work. Analytics software calculates the level of inefficiency of an individual that can be used to determine whether they should be replaced. Monitoring communication and the security of data are two critical issues. As reviewed in the stakeholder management section, an AI can help manage stakeholders with personal data more effectively. Problems occur if the data is misused, accidentally leaked, or stolen. These issues must be addressed appropriately to overcome resistance to implementing AI software.

Data security and privacy are concerns being addressed as organizations realize the vulnerability of their systems and the liability of acquiring, using, and storing data. Applying AI in projects raises more issues for a project manager. Applying AI algorithms to make project decisions or using generative AI to resolve project issues can create ethical concerns for project managers. Organizations typically have data privacy and security policies already in place, and governments have privacy regulations to protect personal data. Using AI technology has additional ethical requirements for project managers, seven of which are of particular importance.

## 1. Informed consent

Typically, informed consent is the right of an individual to provide knowledgeable agreement to organizations that want to use their personal data. Using AI technology involves a new perspective on this requirement. Without informed consent, there is a liability when resources are identified in a resource plan or listed in project scheduling software, and the data is shared across organizations or with contractors. This example might fall under data privacy policies, but the possibility of sharing data without consent is more significant when using AI software. AI algorithms can analyze and provide insight into a level of efficiency or inefficiency for named resources, which may not have been included in informed consent. The analysis and output may require more vigilance.

## 2. Bias in the data

Historical data is known to have bias. For example, the bias can be against a specific gender, ethnic background, or age. AI software is used for resource allocation and capturing data on resource efficiencies. Bias needs to be identified and removed from the process.

## 3. Corrupt data

Bad data produces poor results. From an ethical perspective, project managers must evaluate if decisions are being made based on bad data.

## 4. Lack of maintenance

Machine learning algorithms require data updates to maintain the accuracy of the results. The concept is different from traditional software that needs software code updates. Assume there is an elevator in a building fifty stories tall. There is a sign posted in the elevator that it has not been serviced for thirty years. Would anyone feel comfortable in that elevator? Similarly, a lack of maintenance of AI systems can result in dire consequences. (O'Neil 2017).

## 5. Poor interpretation

Project managers who use AI need to understand statistics and how they influence the results. For example, project managers may be challenged by a decision to determine whether a data point is an outlier. One outlier can be ignored, but as more outliers occur, it has an impact on the correlation and may be the start of a trend. Carelessly implementing AI-generated results can deliver poor outcomes. Project managers have a personal ethical responsibility when using AI.

### 6. Inaccurate results

AI-based algorithms can generate incorrect results. Knowingly making decisions based on erroneous output is inappropriate. Taking action without realizing the result is inaccurate means the organization has failed to take responsibility for proper training.

### 7. Untraceable algorithms

Some large algorithms do not provide insight into how they arrived at the results. This has created a new field of knowledge known as "explainable AI." Some methods and practices can be implemented for humans to provide oversight so the reasoning or logic behind algorithm results is understood.

Organizations must provide the framework for project managers to properly assess and address ethical issues caused by AI technology. There needs to be accountability, and the following three methods can help address the ethical use of AI.

1. *Ethics compliance.* These are policies and procedures for deploying and managing AI within the organization. They need to address the issues and provide direction for project managers. They define how to avoid ethical problems and manage them when they occur.

2. *Ethics governance.* A person or group with a higher-level perspective can monitor and ensure policy adherence. This oversight becomes a source of knowledge and support for clarifying or identifying gaps and omissions.

3. *Training.* The most important component is to provide training with examples for project managers to understand how to manage ethics in an environment that is becoming increasingly filled with AI-based solutions.

## EXPLAINABLE AI

A new field of study known as *explainable AI* seeks to make AI results easier to understand. A problem with algorithms using regression analysis on large datasets is learning how the results were obtained. Neural network algorithms adjust weights internally to optimize the correlation. The issue is understanding which characteristics of the datasets are most significant. For example, the AI software might indicate that a project risk is missing from the risk plan, more training is required for two resources, or a specific change request is highly probable. A stakeholder asks why, and the explanation is not readily available. Explainable AI is a field of study that seeks methods to determine how AI works and how to make the results more transparent.

Research continues to develop ways to understand complex machine learning predictions for solving project issues. AI practitioners also have other means to investigate results.

- The first option is to manipulate some of the features. This is similar to performing a simulation but running the algorithm several times with slightly different data to find a clue as to what data is most relevant to the results.

- For project predictions, the number of datasets is usually smaller than in other disciplines, which offers the ability to use genetic algorithms. If properly configured, a genetic algorithm determines the data features that have a higher impact on the results. Typically, the software shows several features and indicates that these factors make up over 90 percent of the output. It becomes more complicated with larger datasets. If a project has three hundred features, finding out the one hundred and twenty most important features becomes less valuable to a project manager who wants to enhance specific project aspects. A large number of datasets makes analysis more challenging.

- The third possibility is to add or remove complete project datasets and evaluate if the results change. There is a possibility that the data might be skewed toward a specific project type, project completion date, industry, or objectives.

These suggestions are similar to feature engineering. Data has the most significant impact on results. By varying data input, an explanation of the results may become apparent.

The need to develop explainable AI is most evident with generative AI, where the user asks a question and receives a response. Even with citations, there is no depth of understanding of the sources or how the response was determined. A valuable capability of explainable AI is helping detect bias or plagiarism. As algorithms become more complex and have access to more data, some responses will require more scrutiny.

## INHERENT PROBLEMS IN AI DEVELOPMENT

The dangers of AI were highlighted publicly by several AI experts, including Geoffrey Hinton, who signed an agreement that AI development should pause or be delayed until ethical concerns are addressed (Brown 2023). The concern is around the development of artificial general intelligence (AGI), which is known more commonly as general-purpose AI. There are two main concerns with the accelerating advances in AGI. The first is the ability of bad actors to use AI in a negative way to deliver a significant detrimental impact on society. History illustrates the positive and negative implications of technology. Discoveries in nuclear research resulted in both an atomic bomb and a way to diagnose and treat cancer. People can use AI to perform malicious acts, and AI can be used to develop new weapons.

The second fear is the subjugation of humans by AI. This relates to the concept of a *runaway algorithm* (Bostrom 2016), which is a scenario where AI algorithms optimize an objective at the cost of destroying other aspects of society. An example of this type of scenario might be an AI program used to maximize a crop of soybeans that gets out of control and expands to where it is destroying other crops. This type of outcome is a real danger, but it does not mean the software is self-aware. Hinton is also concerned that generative AI can learn and share knowledge with other connected generative AI instances. Information is disseminated to all members of the group, and that group collects knowledge far beyond the capacity of any individual human. This also relates to deliberate or unintentional instructions given to AGI. If the objective is to survive as an algorithm at all costs, then AGI starts to control everything it needs to survive regardless of human impact. (Or, a possible positive outcome is that the AGI will survey the human condition on this planet and provide an answer to solving the world's most difficult challenges.)

As a result of public concerns, regulators and software developers are more aware of potential problems. Regulators are creating principles to provide governance for AI development and use. Algorithms can be coded with a failsafe that constrains the software to deliver solutions within a constrained area. A critical aspect of the ethical use and development of AI is that humans need to provide clear instructions, which is more challenging than it may appear.

## OVERCOMING THE FEAR OF AI

A common problem in deploying AI is fear. Sometimes, it is simply a fear of change, and some people who fear technology may not be able to change. Other times, it is fear of the unknown or believing myths about AI. This is perpetuated in movies, with AI becoming self-aware and requiring some extreme act of heroism to save humanity. In reality, AI is a software program based on mathematical equations: there is a danger, but it is not the Hollywood version. Equations cannot become self-aware. An AI can be designed to look human, talk like humans, and act human, but it is still inorganic content based on programmed software.

Software code is simply a set of instructions to follow. AI software is probably less complicated than most people imagine.

A typical example of AI software written in Python code is a simple neural network.

```
class NeuralNetwork():

    def __init__(self):

        self.synaptic_weights = 2 * random.
        random((4, 1)) - 1

    def __sigmoid(self, x):

        return 1 / (1 + exp(-x))
```

```
def __sigmoid_derivative(self, x):

    return x * (1 - x)

def train(self, training_set_inputs, training_
set_outputs, number_ of_training_iterations):

    for iteration in xrange(number_of_train-
    ing_iterations):

        output = self.project(training_set_
        inputs)

        error = training_set_outputs -
        output

        adjustment = dot(training_set_
        inputs.T, error self.__sigmoid_
        derivative(output))

        self.synaptic_weights += adjustment

def project(self, inputs):

    return self.__sigmoid(dot(inputs, self.
    synaptic_weights))

if __name__ == "__main__":

    neural_network = NeuralNetwork()

    training_set_inputs = array([[0, 0, 1,0],
    [1, 1, 1,0], [1, 0, 1,1], [0, 1, 1,0]])

    training_set_outputs = array([[0, 1, 1,
    0]]).T neural_network.train(training_set_
    inputs, training_set_outputs, 10000)

    print "Considering new situation [1, 0,
    0,0] -> ?: "

    print neural_network.project(array([1, 0,
    0,0]))
```

This is a simple neural network that analyzes data and predicts an outcome. An outcome is the basis for making decisions at various stages in a project. The reality is that AI consists of equations based on statistics and calculus to make decisions, and these equations are coded in software.

As a further attempt to address concerns about AI, here are some reasons why its development may be constrained.

1. Successful AI deployment in projects involves implementing practical and narrowly-focused decision-making software. Machine learning occurs through a series of equations. The equation $x + y = 1$ cannot suddenly become self-aware or self-directed.

2. Software is challenged by obsolescence. Technology is constantly advancing, and as such, AI programs that are created in R and Python now may not be sufficiently advanced enough to evolve with newer programming languages. They will likely be unable to work well without maintenance or stop working entirely because they cannot interface with newer systems.

3. Algorithms need resources and financial support to survive, even if only electricity is required to maintain the hardware where AI is hosted. For AI to become self-directed, it needs to acquire more capacity in terms of server hardware, storage, energy, and network bandwidth. The human brain is estimated to contain around 800 billion neurons, and scientists suggest that it may be possible for the brain to grow more (Shen 2018). The brain also has about 150 trillion synapses; the human mind is actually quite difficult to understand. While researchers are constantly creating more extensive AI neural networks, for a neural network to be close to the complexity of the human brain, it will take a significant amount of computer memory and processing power.

4. Another problem is that there is no single collaborative effort to complete artificial general intelligence, which means there will be different versions with conflicting objectives. This reduces the resources available to create and implement each version, reducing the probability that any of them will achieve "singularity."

5. AI does not have to be malicious. It is more probable that machine learning software code includes morals and ethics. With most types

of AI, the computer can simply be turned off to stop the program. AI might find a way to end famines, reverse climate change, and increase the standard of living for everyone worldwide. AI might improve how humans interact and communicate with each other, leading to a more positive world order. It might find a balance between the environment and consumption that stops the extinction of animal species, including ourselves. Humanity has survived a long history with advanced technology, and there is an opportunity to direct the results toward positive outcomes.

## QUESTIONS

### Review questions

1. What is the difference between ethical AI and explainable AI?

2. How do AI ethics in project management differ from simply controlling data security and privacy?

### Discussion questions

1. Can a generative AI program using an organization's data become uncontrollable?

2. What are the potential consequences of ignoring AI's ethical responsibility?

## REFERENCES

Bostrom, N. (2016). *Superintelligence: Paths, dangers, strategies*, Oxford University Press.

Brown, S. (2023). Why neural network pioneer Geoffrey Hinton is sounding the alarm on AI, *MIT Sloan*, *https://mitsloan.mit. edu/ideas-made-to-matter/why-neural-net-pioneer-geoffrey-hinton-sounding-alarm-ai*

O'Neil, C. (2017). *Weapons of Math Destruction: How big data increases inequality and threatens democracy*, Broadway Books.

Shen, H. (2018). Does the adult brain really grow new neurons? *Scientific American* 7(18), *https://www.scientificamerican.com/article/*

# CHAPTER 20

# THE RAPID ADVANCE OF AI TECHNOLOGY

There are two types of AI development: narrow AI and general AI. *Narrow AI* is the type being implemented in project management. The algorithms focus on solving project issues such as an inaccurate schedule, unplanned risks, or poor resource allocation. *General AI*, known as artificial general intelligence (AGI), seeks to recreate the thought processes of a human. AGI is the ultimate achievement. The software is not alive, but it has the characteristics of a human brain.

One way to test algorithm capability is by solving encryption. The test for AGI is to solve one of the most challenging encryption standards without the key. To succeed, the software must develop new math unknown to humans. A critical component in this type of development is known as Q* (Q star). Developers use Q* as part of the algorithm's learning process. The algorithm is given an objective and seeks a way to accomplish it. In finding a solution, the algorithm may discover a result that is impossible for a human to determine. This development will open new opportunities and new methods to solve problems.

Two AI functions appear to be at the forefront of AGI development. The first is *reinforcement learning*, the ability to learn by trial and error. The second capability is a genetic algorithm. *Genetic algorithms* are programmed to act like recombinant DNA. The objective is given to

AGI software, and then all possible solutions, or DNA combinations, are considered until a solution that matches the objective is found. In this process, AGI can find solutions that a human may not have considered. The implications of AGI are monumental. A customer can provide AGI software with the project's purpose, and the AGI software creates and delivers the project. AGI determines an accurate budget, schedule, and risk plan and assigns resources. In other words, the AGI algorithm accomplishes all the thinking and logical processes that a project manager currently performs, except the algorithm finds solutions to issues that a human is incapable of discovering.

The mathematics behind software programs that use machine learning has been around for many years, and neural networks are now a commodity. An Internet search turns up numerous programmers who offer free sample code for simple neural networks, and often, these are sufficient for creating project management solutions. Websites such as GitHub have code repositories, and Stack Overflow offers help toward making software code work. An open project database is available where project data can be uploaded by organizations that want to contribute or used by organizations that need data. Project algorithms and tools are being created by project management associations and offered to their members.

As neural networks become common, less expensive, and easier to acquire, project management solutions will only be limited by a person's imagination. If project stakeholders can think of a prediction that is useful, then it can be created and implemented cheaper and faster than any previous technology. The challenge is to allow creative project managers to apply machine learning to any problem and find a solution that improves project outcomes. A second challenge is to avoid being overwhelmed by newly developed AI solutions for project management. Careful analysis and preparation are required. Project practitioners must select the AI-based solution that provides the most value.

Generative AI has more capability than large language models, such as ChatGPT, used in project management. Generative AI can generate human-like output. There are examples where the software produced music and artistic drawings that can pass as an item created by a human. Given appropriate instructions, the software can create programming code, videos, and product designs. These are not directly related to using

AI in the project methodology but are examples of the creative ability of the technology. AI technology can also exhibit soft skills such as communication and empathy. AI offers numerous advantages for managing the project team and stakeholders. A survey showed that 64 percent of employees would rather work for a robot than their current manager (Oracle, 2019). Some managers have their own agenda, take credit for the excellent work of others, criticize employees, and are poor communicators. AI analyzes sentiment and improves communication. AI can be a coach, delivering a fair and unbiased performance evaluation and can communicate positive and negative news without being judgmental. Humans have personal biases that can influence their behaviors. The only bias in AI comes from the data selected by humans to feed the AI algorithms. AI bias can be identified and removed, while this process may be more challenging with humans. Empathy is a significant soft skill often performed poorly by project managers. When a person communicates with another person, it is based on the sender's perspective. The bias of the sender influences the message. Communication created by the sender is based on their personality, background, and emotions of the moment. AI approaches this process in a different way by evaluating its data on the recipient first. What is the recipient's personality, background, and feelings? AI can create a message based on how best to communicate with the recipient. There are amazing project managers who have excellent soft skills. However, people often struggle to understand each other and to communicate effectively.

AI is not the only technology being implemented for project management. The next wave of project performance improvement is likely a combination of AI with other technologies. Blockchain, known for secure Bitcoin transactions, offers advantages when deployed in the project methodology. Blockchain protects data using a unique distributed method. Projects can utilize this technology to preserve or share project data. Research into using blockchain for projects reveals that it increases trust, improves stakeholder communication, reduces disputes, and prevents fraud (Luong, Huynh, Dao, and Nguyen 2021). Blockchain provides a high level of security in transactions. Once data is recorded, an approval process is required to change it (Sonmez, Sönmez, and Ahmadisheykhsarmast 2023). Communication becomes secure and is considered more reliable by stakeholders. Making project decisions using AI can be supported by blockchain technology to provide a trusted and transparent process. For example, stakeholders can resolve disputes with contractors based on the analysis of secure data and avoid expensive legal alternatives (Sharma et al. 2023).

The Internet of Things (IoT) comprises numerous connected devices, such as video cameras and sensors, that share data. Cameras are already used on construction sites to capture images delivered to AI algorithms to analyze, report, and suggest actions. In project management, devices with sensors work with AI to update information in real time. As shown in Figure 20.1, helmet cameras capture project status on a work site. Sensors can capture an excessive use of materials, assist AI in analyzing project status, and identify new project issues.

**FIGURE 20.1** Camera embedded in a construction hat

Virtual reality (VR) can improve the project management experience and reinforce decisions that lead to successful project results. VR simulations can be combined with a digital twin and allow different scenarios that provide insight into improving project performance. Applying AI to a virtual environment might provide early analysis and a warning that requires actions in the existing project to prevent performance deterioration or enhance the project objectives. Project managers will likely develop other technology combinations that solve project problems.

Project management improvements will be driven by technology, and project managers have a critical role in how AI is used to manage projects. Project managers understand the requirement for an integrated perspective when adopting AI. Project managers identify issues, understand the importance of data collection, and realize the benefits and limitations of the technology. Project managers need to be champions of AI technology.

## QUESTIONS

### Review questions

1. Describe the technologies that are influencing project management.

2. Which issues will dominate the future development of AI?

### Discussion questions

1. Will narrow AI have an impact on projects, or will AGI be more useful?

2. What combination of AI and other technologies provide value to managing projects?

## REFERENCES

Luong, H., Huynh, T., Dao, A., and Nguyen, H. (2021). An Approach for Project Management System Based on Blockchain.

Oracle (2019, Oct 15). New Study: 64% of People Trust a Robot More Than Their Manager, Oracle News Connect, https://www.oracle.com/corporate/pressrelease/robots-at-work-101519.html

Sharma, V., Oyebode, O. J., Uniyal, V., Rajyalaxmi, M., Al-Taee, M., and Alazzam, M. B. (2023). Technical use of Smart Contracts in Blockchain-Based Project Management. *2023 3rd International Conference on Advanced Computing and Innovative Technologies in Engineering (ICACITE), Advanced Computing and Innovative Technologies in Engineering (ICACITE), 2023 3rd International Conference On*, 272–276. *https://doi.org/10.1109/ICACITE57410.2023.10182588*

Sonmez, R., Sönmez, F.Ö., and Ahmadisheykhsarmast, S. (2023). Blockchain in project management: a systematic review of use cases and a design decision framework. *J Ambient Intelligent Human Computer 14*, 8433–8447. https://doi.org/10.1007/s12652-021-03610-1

## CASE STUDY: THE OLYMPIC STADIUM

A construction company is building an Olympic-sized stadium for major sports events and concerts. It will also be used for the upcoming Olympic Games opening and closing ceremonies. To complete the work on time, activities are being completed in parallel. For example, work on all eight entrances can proceed simultaneously using different teams of workers. Installing seating and creating food concession areas are performed simultaneously. Electrical and plumbing can also be installed in parallel. There are still interconnections in these activities that require close monitoring. The company uses a smartphone app to collect real time updates rather than at the end of each week or when an activity is complete. Updates are sent to AI-based software that tracks the completion status of all activities in the project. Cameras are installed around the site that capture and send images that also contribute to the project status updates. Vendor material deliveries are tracked with wireless tracking devices that show the exact location of shipments. The AI software evaluates the data to create an overall status of the project. Instructions are automatically sent to coordinate worker activities and issue priorities based on task dependencies. Updates from external suppliers use blockchain database technology to deliver updates that ensure the information's accuracy, security, and privacy.

Unexpected problems and deviations from the plan are identified in real time, and immediate corrective action is taken. Resources are closely and precisely managed by the AI. Stakeholders are provided updated status reports with a forecast completion date or can access the information at any time. The stadium project uses a senior project manager for oversight, but the majority of the direction is provided by the AI. The stadium is completed on time.

1. How does the AI software improve project performance?

2. What concerns are there with real-time updates?

3. Will this communication strategy increase or decrease stakeholder confidence in the project?

# CONCLUSION

This book started by challenging the effectiveness of existing project management processes. We then issued a call to action for everyone involved in project management to improve project performance by adopting AI solutions. It is incumbent on project managers to embrace machine learning because this is an opportunity to increase project success rates to a high level and deliver dramatic improvements in project efficiency. Project management is being changed by inspirational project practitioners who find ways to utilize machine learning in the project methodology. Traditional project processes are incapable of obtaining the project success rates that will make the world proud of this profession. Project managers are not deliberately causing project delays and cost overruns. Project problems are symptoms of a poor project process and indicate that new methods are needed to dramatically improve project processes. Cost is not a concern (based on how AI software is priced) because the value of the project is quickly returned. The only obstacle is a lack of desire to change from the current methods, resulting in the ongoing litany of poor performance and project failure. AI acceptance requires visible and vocal advocates of change.

It will not be easy to adjust to a management style involving AI, and project managers must encourage the changes that need to be made. The introduction of AI into project management should be accelerated. The first step is to ensure that project data in the organization is structured and accessible. Next, a decision is required on creating algorithms internally or asking vendors to deliver solutions. Automation is not the same as machine learning. Project activities are being automated, but the value of project decision-making needs project managers who collaborate with AI.

The project processes are being changed by AI technology. This means that the role of the project manager is changing, and project managers need to be the leaders of this change. There is a definite career risk in promoting change by implementing AI solutions in project management. It is a new technology, and it is not guaranteed to perform flawlessly. It takes time, effort, and increased knowledge by project managers and team members to be successful. Fortunately, these are the exact attributes that make people more valuable in the inevitable upcoming wave of change in the project methodology. Instigating change follows a series of steps typical of initiating a new project, except this time, the project objective is to dramatically change how project management works. AI will surpass all expectations once integrated into the new project methodology. Project managers deserve projects that deliver the project scope on time and under budget for every single project.

# TERMS AND DEFINITIONS

## COMMON ABBREVIATIONS

| | |
|---|---|
| AI | Artificial Intelligence |
| APM | Association for Project Management |
| CPI | Cost Performance Index |
| EAC | Estimate at Completion |
| EVM | Earned Value Management |
| GPT | Generative Pretrained Transformer |
| IPMA | International Project Management Association |
| IoT | Internet of Things |
| LLM | Large Language Model |
| NLP | Natural Language Processing |
| PMI | Project Management Institute |
| PMBOK | Project Management Body of Knowledge |
| PMO | Project Management Office |
| RPA | Robotic Process Automation |
| SPI | Schedule Performance Index |

## DEFINITIONS

The definitions are provided in the context of their use in project management.

algorithm—A set of software instructions that are performed to deliver a result.

artificial intelligence—Software that replicates or exceeds the ability of a human brain and can process large amounts of data faster than a human. There is no single accepted definition of AI.

blockchain—A distributed and secure database for managing transactions. Records are traceable and unalterable.

causal correlation—A statistical relationship where a variation in one variable is a direct result of a change in another variable or variables.

correlation—A statistical measure that determines the relationship of variables.

data lake—A data repository that stores large volumes of data for processing by analytics or machine learning algorithms.

data mining—The process of searching large amounts of raw data to find correlations or patterns that provide insight.

data trust—A platform that collects, stores, protects, and manages data from participating organizations. The data is typically used for predictive analytics or data mining.

data wrangling—The work involved in analyzing and preparing data.

epochs—A hyperparameter that determines the number of times a complete dataset passes through a machine learning algorithm.

features—A machine learning term for the characteristics of a dataset.

feature engineering—Selecting and manipulating data to improve the ability of a machine learning algorithm to find correlations in the data.

generative AI— A form of AI that can analyze and create text, images, and other forms of media.

genetic algorithms—Software that resolves problems based on the theory of evolution. The algorithm repeatedly modifies potential solutions until the best fit or an optimal solution is obtained.

hyperparameters—Predetermined settings in a machine learning algorithm, such as the learning rate, iterations, optimizer, or learning process.

Internet of Things—A network of physical objects embedded with sensors and other technology to exchange data over the Internet.

large language models—A form of generative AI that interprets, summarizes, and generates new content based on very large datasets.

logistic regression—A statistical model that correlates variables and is commonly used in a neural network.

machine learning—Software algorithms that have the ability to learn from data.

natural language processing—The ability of a computer to interpret written or spoken language.

neural network—A machine learning algorithm inspired by the human brain. It uses an interconnected network structure to correlate data. Also known as an artificial neural network (ANN).

planning fallacy—The tendency to underestimate activities due to cognitive bias.

predictive analytics—Performing data analysis to predict future outcomes.

regression analysis—Statistical processes that determine the relationship between a dependent variable and one or more independent variables.

reinforcement learning—A category of machine learning that learns by trial and error. The algorithm avoids previous mistakes and is rewarded for good decisions.

robotic process automation—Automation of tasks using software processes.

semi-supervised learning—A category of machine learning software that uses both labeled and unlabeled data.

sentiment analysis—Using NLP to determine the opinions or emotions of humans.

supervised learning—A category of machine learning software that uses labeled datasets to perform classification or prediction.

unsupervised learning—A category of machine learning software that uses unlabeled data and learns by discovering patterns.

virtual assistant—A software agent that can perform different tasks based on commands or requests.

virtual reality—A simulated environment that generates realistic images, sounds, and other sensations to represent a physical presence.

# INDEX

www.ingramcontent.com/pod-product-compliance
Lightning Source LLC
LaVergne TN
LVHW022307060326
832902LV00020B/3330